GU00983540

EAT-JAPAN
JAPANESE FOOD
DIRECTORY   Vol.1

Cross Media Ltd.

66 Wells Street, London W1T 3PY UK
Tel : +44 (0)20 7436 1960
Fax: +44 (0)20 7436 1930
www.eat-japan.com (Eat-Japan)
www.redbooks.net (Red Directory)
Email: info@eat-japan.com

(ATTENTION)

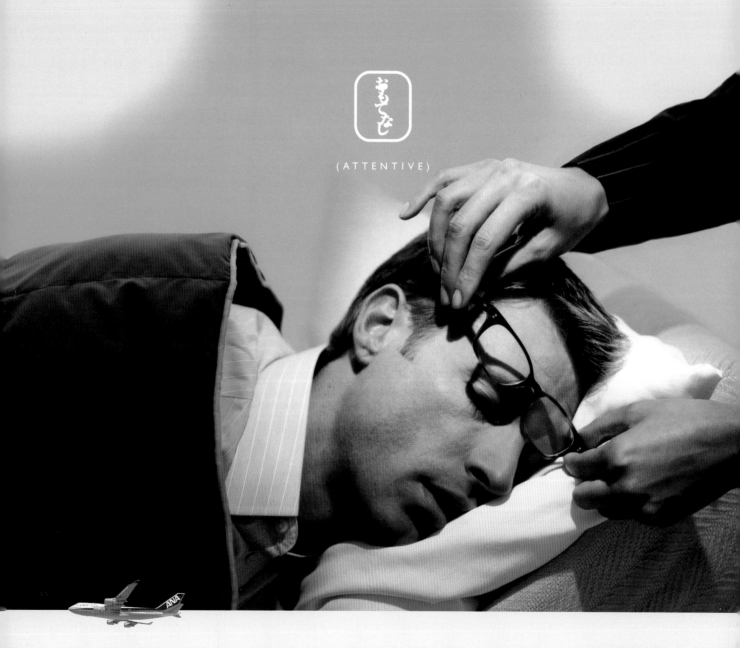

(ATTENTIVE)

Whether it's a blanket that feels a touch warmer or a meal that arrives a little hotter, ANA's meticulously attentive Japanese service will make your flight as comfortable as possible. Even if you're not awake to appreciate it.

ENJOYED DAILY TO JAPAN AND ASIA.

A STAR ALLIANCE MEMBER ✦ ™

www.ana-europe.com

Contents

IFE
International
Food
and
Drink Exhibition

2003

A look at the UK's No.1 International Food Event and its Japanese Pavilion

This year's IFE will be the biggest ever, featuring an incredible range of food, drink and related products from all around the world.

Not only is the biannual IFE a great opportunity for people in the food industry to exchange ideas, make contacts and do business, it is also an absolutely essential event for food fans, with a wonderful array of delicious food and drink on offer from England and countries all around the world. The event also includes a great variety of activities and demonstrations, and seminars and debates on a broad range of food and food industry related topics. In its 24-year history the IFE has established an international reputation, and in 2001 it was moved from its traditional home in Earls Court to the purpose-built ExCel exhibition centre in Docklands, London's largest single-site exhibition venue. The spacious ExCel, with its modern facilities, impressive Dockside location, and close proximity to London City Airport, is perfect for what the exhibition has become. IFE 2001 saw the addition of a Japanese pavilion featuring 29 stands, and over 90 companies. IFE 2003 (23rd to the 26th of March) will also include, for the first time, exhibitors from Brazil, Australia and Malaysia, as well as pavilions from Spain, Italy, France, Canada, the USA, and a New World Pavilion featuring products from as far afield as South Africa, New Zealand and Mexico. This year's exhibition will also feature increased representation from Scotland, Northern Ireland and Wales, and of course, the very best of British food. So, whether food is your business, your passion, or both, whatever your taste, IFE has plenty to get stuck into.

A Report on the Massive Success of IFE 2001

– An International Exhibition that boasted a whole lot to eat and drink, a whole lot of people well worth meeting and much, much more.

With an incredible range of international food and drink and food related products from a total of 1,360 exhibitors from 41 countries, IFE 2001 attracted over 26,000 visitors including major UK and European buyers.

IFE 2001 was quite simply a huge success and general feedback from both visitors and exhibitors was excellent. According to Lisa Tompkins, Event Director of IFE Organisers Fresh RM: "We exceeded our objective of attracting a high level of quality buyers, senior managers and international visitors ... Major European supermarket buyers were present, including buying teams from the major national multiples, catering groups and manufactures, including trading and purchasing directors. ExCel and our contracters were extremely helpful and their dedication ensured that we were able to achieve a high standard at the show." The success of IFE 2001 was greatly contributed to by its venue, the newly built ExCel centre in Docklands, which impressed both exhibitors and visitors with its size, convenient layout and state of the art facilities, and was much easier to navigate and generally far better suited to the event than its previous location in Earls Court. The exhibition was divided into 12 separate product sections: Bakery and Confectionery, Frozen Foods, Seafood, Organic and fresh Produce, Cheese and Dairy, Food Packaging and Design, Alcoholic and Soft Drinks, National and International Pavilions, E-business Solutions, Speciality Food From Britain, and two General Food and Drink sections. As well as these sections there were also two lounges, a club room, a total of six cafes and restaurants and an Innovation Zone for seminars, demonstrations and debates etc.

The very best of British food was displayed in abundance, from chocolate and ice cream to smoked fish and fine cheeses. On display were soups from The Real Soup Company, cheeses from Wensleydale Creamery, and such delicacies as kiln-roast salmon and smoked duck breast from Dartmouth Smokehouse to mention just a few of the items from a wonderful variety of both traditional and innovative foods. There was also a major presence from the British Meat Council who invited visitors to recover traditional British meat cooking methods such as the slow cooking of inexpensive cuts, and fought back against health scares with scientific reassurances and new beef recipe suggestions for caterers. Companies such as Bombay Bangers, and the Curry Sauce Company were also present, demonstrating Britain's long standing association with Indian culture. And as well as the section solely devoted to British speciality foods, those of Scotland, Wales, Northern Ireland and various regional groups appeared in their own pavilions.

For the first time in IFE's history there was a Japanese national pavilion to show off some of that great nation's edible treasures. The pavilion was organised by the Japanese Government and JETRO, the Japan External Trade Organisation, which promotes and supports trade between Japan and the rest of the world, and included over 90 companies showcasing a broad selection of their unique products. Food and drink included among other things sake and shochu (clear spirit), confectioneries, pickles, savoury snacks and sushi ingredients. Apart from Japanese foods, which are relatively speaking quite well known in the UK such as sushi and tofu, visitors

'At international trade exhibitions in the past, Japan has been more concerned with introducing itself as an unfamiliar culture rather than actually actively trading, but here things were different…'

had an opportunity to sample such specialised products as the fragrant and once extremely rare maitake mushroom and natto (fermented soybeans), and there were green teas, sakes and Yakult's fruit and vegetable juices and fermented milk health drinks on offer to wash down these gourmet foods. In the past at international trade exhibitions Japan has been more concerned with introducing itself as an unfamiliar culture rather than actually actively trading but here things were different. The Japanese companies were geared up for business and many had more than 100 business enquiries, quite a number of which led to subsequent deals.

The exhibition also featured such varied international specialties as pancake mixes and pretzels from the USA, beer and vodka from Canada, ham from France, cheeses from Italy, fine fruit juices from Germany, and a truly awesome array of other foods from European countries and around the world (unfortunately far too many, and from far too many places to possibly mention in this piece). But apart from the mouth-watering exhibits on display, at the exhibition's Innovation Zone there was also a broad range of demonstrations, seminars and debates on topics such as organic food certification and trade, cheese marketing and the revitalisation of pubs with 'revolutionary foods' as well as 'Business Breakfasts' with titles like 'The Future of Food Purchasing'. At these sessions professionals from many different areas of the food industry dispensed valuable information in what amounted to a mini university of food studies! All in all, the event went about as far as it is possible to go towards covering international food and opening doors to food business in four days, and the memory of the 2001 event whets the appetite for IFE 2003 and beyond.

IFE 2003 - a look at just a few examples of what to expect from this year's exhibition.

Over 1,400 companies will be exhibiting their products at IFE 2003 and the increased number of nations participating in the event means a broader range of foods than ever before. Furthermore, in addition to all the established traditions, for this year's exhibition (held at the ExCel centre from the 23rd to the 26th of March) a selection of new features will be on offer for retailers and independents. For example the new Retail Buyers Club, which gives access to a central display of products in the New Products Display Area, and an Independent's Day tour around the exhibition as well as an information guide on relevant exhibitors and product samples. The Theatre of Cheese will feature tutored tastings, demonstrations and seminars on commercial issues facing retailers and offer tips on cross merchandising and making the most of cheese displays on deli-counters from industry experts. At this year's show, many new companies will be exhibiting alongside those of long standing with IFE. First time exhibitor Jim Conlin, Sales and Marketing director of A Camacho UK, said: "As a company new to the UK, we are delighted to be exhibiting at IFE 2003. The Show is the ideal place for our full range of branded own-label products to be seen by both UK and international buyers." And Tim Barlow, Managing director of G. Costa, commented; "IFE is one of the key shows in the international calendar and we are looking forward to returning to showcase our new products and existing portfolio to the major industry figures". Reviewing the previous show and with the new additions, it looks like the IFE will indisputably prove itself, once again, to be the UK international food event.

The Japan Pavilion
– a rainbow of tastes from the Land of the Rising Sun.

The introduction of the Japan Pavilion at IFE 2001 provided an opportunity for westerners to get intimate with the elements of a unique and sophisticated cuisine which just keeps growing in international popularity. Here's a taste of what to expect from Japan at IFE 2003.

1 Kiku-Masamune Sake Brewing Co., Ltd.

Kiku-Masamune Sake Brewing Co., Ltd. began when the Kano family started producing sake (rice wine) in Mikage, Kobe in 1659. The company first exported to Britain in 1877, and now exports sake, made under its motto 'Quality First', to the USA, Europe and worldwide.

2 Domer, Inc.

In 1995, Domer began producing pre-germinated whole rice in Ueda in Nagano Prefecture. Pre-germinated whole rice makes it tastier and easier to cook, and because of the activation of dormant enzymes, far more nutritious. It is used to treat a range of ailments including Alzheimer's disease.

3 Waner Inc.

Waner Inc. (Kinjirushi brand) is famous for pioneering the production of both powdered wasabi (Japanese horseradish) and wasabi paste. The company was founded in 1930 by Mr. Kobayashi, who dedicated his life to developing and popularising wasabi products that, over the years, have won many awards.

4 Harizuka Nosan

Founded by Toju Harizuka, who is famous as an agriculturist, Harizuka Nosan carefully considers both human health and the natural environment in the production process of its nutritious pickled vegetables, which starts with chemical fertiliser-free soil. Its pickles have been favourably received at worldwide exhibitions, including IFE 2001.

5 Choya Umeshu Co., Ltd.

Choya begun as a winery in 1914, and is now the world's No.1 manufacturer of umeshu (a liqueur made from ume plums), both in terms of quantity and quality. Choya's umeshu are made using only natural ingredients and the highest quality ume, a fruit rich with health-giving properties.

6 Mitsukan Group Corporation

Mitsukan produces a range of quality Japanese vinegars for both catering and domestic use. For example, 'Shiragiku', a mellow tasting distilled rice vinegar, is perfect for use in many Japanese dishes and 'Yusen', a slowly fermented dark coloured 'full body sake cake vinegar', is used in making sushi rice.

7 Kairinmaru Beer Co., Ltd.

Kairinmaru's award-winning frozen sushi (First Prize, Hokkaido Processed Food Fair 2001) is the most popular variety in Japan and completely free from chemical additives and its 100% buckwheat instant frozen soba noodles are not only convenient and delicious, but also extremely good for you.

8 Miyasaka Brewery Co., Ltd.

Originally producing only sake, in 1916 Miyasaka began using its advanced fermentation experience to use in the making of miso (fermented soy bean paste). Today it produces a range of misos and instant miso soups to suit all tastes and requirements as well as freeze dried ingredients.

– The Japan Pavilion –
No. 3217, 3314

9 Miyasaka Brewing Co., Ltd.

Since its founding in 1662 at the foot of the Kirigamine highlands in Nagano Prefecture, Miyasaka's Masumi brewery has steadily perfected the art of sake brewing. The superior 'Yeast #7' was discovered at the brewery in 1946, and is now used by over 60% of the nation's sake breweries.

10 Fukui Seimen Co., Ltd.

Located in the beautiful Echizen area, Fukui Seimen produces high quality soba, udon and ramen noodles using its own patented technology and healthy ingredients. Its handmade noodles were already highly regarded by local restaurants when it began producing for domestic use in 1988.

11 Yamajirushi Miso

Since its founding in the Nagano Prefecture, a district famous for miso, in 1955, Yamajirushi Miso has been producing fine misos and seasonings with a high regard for human health and the environment. In 1976 it established a subsidiary company in California, thus beginning its global expansion.

12 Tomen Foods UK Ltd.

Founded in 1920, Tomen Corporation deals in, as well as textiles and metals, foodstuffs such as wasabi, pickled ginger, nori seaweed and chocolate snacks. It also offers Sohana brand Junmai Ginjo sake, which is traditionally and labour intensively brewed and famously enjoyed by the Japanese imperial family.

13 Royce' Confect Co., Ltd.

Since 1983, Royce' Confect Co., Ltd. has been manufacturing superior chocolate in Hokkaido in an ideal environment, blessed with clean air and natural spring water. Since then, the company has developed a range of luxury 'Nama' chocolates, and has branched out to produce cookies and other snacks.

14 Shimodozono International GmbH

Shimodozono produces a range of exceptionally high quality certified organic green teas grown using sophisticated cultivation methods in the ideal conditions of Kagoshima in southern Kyushu. Marketed under the 'Keiko' brand name, these teas have a fresh and distinctive taste and highly aromatic scent.

15 Asahi Beer Europe Ltd.

'Asahi Super Dry' is Japan's biggest-selling beer, and also brewed in the Czech Republic, it is now becoming popular among young Europeans. The Ashai Breweries Group also offers a range of shochu (clear spirit) including 'Ichiban-fuda', an authentic shochu made from 100% wheat.

16 Yamato Soysauce & Miso Co., Ltd.

Yamato was founded in 1911 in the harbour town of Ono in Ishikawa Prefecture, a region famous for rice. It produces soy sauce, miso, rice vinegar, nori seaweed, wasabi and other traditional foods using locally grown organic rice, organic soy beans mainly from Hokkaido and other healthy, natural ingredients.

Sushi Eggs Benedict
Maggie Thurer, Grand Winner

The Original Sushi Competition
- the birth of a brand-new cuisine.

The first Original Sushi Competition in 2002
was a great success and this year's competition, now well underway,
looks set to be even greater.

The Nation that has most enthusiastically adopted sushi so far is America, which has over 2,000 Japanese restaurants in the state of California alone. Just as they did with pizza, the Americans have played around with sushi resulting in new forms such as the legendary California Roll. Over the past few years in Britain sushi's popularity has grown rapidly and now it seems that it's our turn to play with this rich, varied and delicious cuisine. And as Original Sushi 2002 showed, we're not at all bad at it! The Original Sushi Competition was the brainchild of Mr. Kazuhiro Marumo, Managing Director of Cross Media (publisher of Eat-Japan magazine), who developed the concept with Mr. Kunihiro Kondo, Managing Director of Matsuri Restaurant Group (a subsidurary company of Central Japan Railway Co). The competition was founded, in the words of Mr. Kondo, who was head of its committee in 2002, as: "an effort to combine the imagination and ingredients of the West with centuries of traditional Japanese cuisine to inspire a totally new sushi, a British sushi."

www.sushi-competition.com

Anthony Nott

Supported by

EMBASSY OF JAPAN    Japan National Tourist Organisation   JETRO
Japan External Trade Organization

The First Annual Original Sushi Competition – The Birth of British Sushi

The competition asked entrants to use their imaginations and come up with original sushi recipes using any ingredients they liked as long as they included sushi rice. People of many different ages, ethnicities and backgrounds all living in the UK took part, sending in over 500 recipes many of which were both beautiful and delicious.

The final event was held in March at the Matsuri St. James's restaurant in London's West End, which was packed to capacity with contestants (a significant number of which were children, largely as a result of an Original Sushi Mini-Event held at Henwick primary school in Eltham at which pupils had fun learning about and tasting sushi before being invited to enter the competition,) press, and guests including the Japanese Ambassador Mr. Orita, and representatives of Japanese sponsor companies. Speeches were made by Mr. Kondo, the head of the competition's committee and the Ambassador before one by one, the finalists' dishes were brought out from the kitchen and displayed. Then, while around 200 guests and contestants mingled and chatted, the judges began to scrutinize, nibble and discuss. When the moment of truth came, Chair of the judges Lesley Waters (from the BBC's Ready Steady Cook!), and the other five judges on the panel, which included professional sushi chefs, challenged by the extremely high standard of the finalists' entries that a decision on the winners was very difficult to reach. Eventually the award ceremony took place over an hour behind schedule, and in her speech afterwards, Ms. Waters spoke of the significance of the event and how honoured she felt to have been involved.

The grand winner!   Sushi Calendar 2003

The Sushi Gallery

The term 'British sushi' indicated only the place where the recipes originated and imposed no limits whatsoever on their influences, which reflected the multicultural nature of the U.K. today. Thanks to the expert preparations by Mr. Kurokawa, one of the Matsuri chefs, the finalists' dishes looked simply wonderful. Guests wandered around gazing at sushi so beautiful in appearance that it posed the question 'eat or frame?' Artistic edibles or edible art? For most of the guests it was only a visual treat as tasting the wares was the privilege of the judges (and a few lucky members of the press!) but fortunately there were other sushi dishes, snacks and drinks available for the guests, so looking at the art didn't become too mouth-wateringly painful. Bronze, Silver, and Gold Prizes were awarded for the adult and children's categories, as well as a Chef's Prize, a Chair of Judges' Prize, and an overall Grand Winner. The title of Grand Winner (and the prize of a trip for two to Japan!) went to Maggie Thurer for her beautiful and delicious 'Sushi Eggs Benedict' - a gourmet dish consisting of poached quail's egg and smoked salmon on rice topped with hollandaise sauce. Ms. Naomi Hattori and her 'Italian Sushi' took the Adult's Gold' - her recipe consisted of rice wrapped in seaweed, topped with chopped tomatoes, mozzarella cheese and secured with a seaweed strip and served with a mayonnaise and

SPONSORS

'I Love the UK' Sushi
Seiko Kitano (age 10), Children's Gold winner

Sweet Berry Sushi
Emma Garderton, Adult Bronze winner

Parma Ham Wrapping Sushi
Somparat Srisantisuk, Finalist

Fishy Dishy
Jake McEnroe (age 10), Children's Bronze winner

miso sauce. The Gold in the children's category went to Seiko Kitano (aged 10) for her 'I love The UK' Sushi – a visual and culinary treat made up of rice, and topped with fried lemon sole and asparagus spears and secured with a seaweed strip and served with a mayonnaise and miso sauce. These dishes and others from the competitions finalists were collected in a calendar made to celebrate the wonderful new dishes, and, as each dish was accompanied by its recipe, gave people the chance to make and enjoy the dishes themselves (if you want to get your hands on these recipes 'Original Sushi Calendar 2003' is still available from www.eat-japan.com). If you're eager to try some British sushi, some of the finalists' recipes are available as a selection plate at the Matsuri St. James's restaurant (who knows, perhaps one of them will become Britain's answer to the California Roll!) but why not go even further and create some British sushi. You may be too late to enter Original Sushi' 2003, but the final event of the competition is open to the public and is the perfect place to go to find inspiration for your own masterpiece to unleash upon the world at the next competition!

> "'British sushi' indicated only the place where the recipes originated and imposed no limits whatsoever on their influences."

Original Sushi' 2003 – The Future of British Sushi

Building on the success of the first Original Sushi Competition last year, Original Sushi' 2003 is being organised to allow a cultural exchange to take place between Japan and the rest of the world as represented by those living in the UK, as well as to introduce completely new forms of sushi. In the words of this year's competition's committee head, Mr. Makoto Kakebayashi (Director General of JETRO London): "The first Original Sushi Competition showed that Western ingredients and the imaginations of the people of the UK could be combined with the Japanese traditional cuisine of sushi to create wonderful new dishes. The 2003 competition is going to be another genuine cultural exchange and also a lot of fun." The competition's final event is being held on April the 8th (see www.sushi-competition.com for details) at Matsuri High Holborn, the Matsuri Restaurant Group's second restaurant which opened in October 2002, and several Original Sushi Mini Events have been organised in the run up to the event,

Spanish Sushi
Nathan Middlemiss, Adult Silver winner

Italian Sushi
Naomi Hattori, Adult Gold winner

Tuti Sushi Cake
Katherine Dar (age 11), Chair of Judge's Prize

Sushi for My Greedy Dad
Yui Sumitomo (age 7), Children's Silver winner

perhaps the most important of which is to be held at Le Cordon Bleu London Culinary Arts Institute. Le Cordon Bleu is one of the World's most prestigious culinary institutes and has branches worldwide. This event will be attended by tutors, students, and ex-students now working as professional chefs. There will also be events held at Hall School Wimbledon in South West London for its pupils aged 10 to 12 and their parents and at the Brighton branch of 'Moshi Moshi Sushi' (the popular 'conveyer-belt' sushi restaurant chain, for local primary school pupils, their parents, and local cookery school students as well as the media. At the time of writing, other possible venues are still being discussed. These Mini Events will feature appearances and demonstrations from expert 'decorative sushi artists' from the All Japan Sushi Association, who have developed the visual element of the form to breath-taking levels of beauty with a range incredibly complex, subtle and varied designs such as animals and birds, flowers, and cartoon characters as well as abstract patterns. These edible works of art are made entirely from traditional sushi ingredients such

> "The 2003 competition is going to be another genuine cultural exchange and also a lot of fun."
>
> Mr. Kakebayashi,
> Competition Committee Head.

as fish, vegetables and seaweed and the arrangement and their presentation is yet another dimension of their art. As well as publicizing the competition, the Mini Events will allow people to learn about the history and variety of the cuisine and try their hand at making it and tasting it themselves. Both the organizers of the competition and the guest sushi artists feel it is very important that sushi is introduced to children and young people whose imaginations and receptivity could well play a key role in the future evolution of new forms of the cuisine. This year's competition is being sponsored by; ANA, a leading Japanese airline; Asahi Beer, producers of Japan's biggest selling beer; Kikkoman, the world's leading soy sauce producer; Kewpie Mayonnaise, Japan's leading mayonnaise producer and; Matsuri Restaurant Group, all of which add prestige to the competition as do the Embassy of Japan (London); JETRO (Japan External Trade Organization) and JNTO (Japan National Tourist Organisation). To sum up, last year's competition gave birth to British sushi, and Original Sushi 2003 is sure to take it even further, perhaps even as far as your own kitchen table!

NAGOYA
–The heart of Japan

Exploring the sights, culture and culinary specialities of Nagoya and the surrounding area

The city of Nagoya, capital of Aichi prefecture, is the birthplace of three of the country's most famous warriors and was one of the great castle towns of the Edo period. Home today to the world-famous Toyota Motor Corporation, it is also a place where traditional craftsmen and women can still feel at home.

Miso, a paste made with soybeans, rice or barley, is a staple diet of the Japanese, and one of the most popular brand names is *hatcho miso*, a soybean-based variety which originated in Aichi during the early Edo period.

Historical Aichi is also looking towards the future, as it gears up to host the 2005 World Exposition. Preparations for the global event are already well underway, and Japan's newest international airport is due to open for business here just over two years from now.

Ramsey Zarifeh

Ramsey Zarifeh's new book, *Japan by Rail*, published by Trailblazer, is a practical and user-friendly guide to travelling around Japan, with sightseeing tips and advice on where to eat and sleep. Available in bookstores or on the web at www.trailblazer-guides.com.

Nagoya Noh Theatre

Hatchomiso no Sato

A trip to Nagoya
- the city that never sleeps

Exploring the sights, sounds and flavours of Aichi's capital

Stepping back in time

The origins of modern-day Nagoya, as the regional and economic capital of central Japan, can be traced back at least several centuries to the founding of Nagoya Castle in 1612. Japan's most celebrated warlord, Tokugawa Ieyasu, gave the order for the castle to be constructed as a secure base along the main Tokaido Highway linking the ancient imperial capital, Kyoto, with the city of Edo (present-day Tokyo). The original castle walls may be long gone, but the 1959 reconstruction is celebrated for its roof-top pair of glittering gold dolphins.

One of the best times to visit the castle – which houses a collection of artefacts dating back to the Edo period - is in spring, when the 20th century building is surrounded by over 2,000 cherry blossom trees in full bloom. Though the castle is

dwarfed today by the gleaming skyscrapers of downtown Nagoya, it's nevertheless easy to imagine how impressive and foreboding it must have been when the fortification first appeared on the city skyline nearly 400 years ago.

Visitors to Nagoya can step back in time to a bygone era by wandering along nearby Shikemichi, a long stretch of traditional wooden merchant homes, warehouses and shrines along the Horikawa canal which winds its way towards the castle. Don't leave the castle grounds without visiting Nagoya's very own 630-seat Noh theatre, built in 1997. The elegant, Japanese-style building houses a small exhibition dedicated to Noh, a classical form of stylised theatre which dates back more than 600 years. Performances are held here on a seasonal basis and tickets are always in high demand.

High on the list of any historical tour of latter-day Nagoya should also be the Tokugawa Art Museum, which boasts a collection of more than 10,000 treasures that once belonged to the Owari branch of the Tokugawa family which ruled Japan from 1603 to 1867. Look out for items such as glittering swords and genuine pieces of armour, utensils used in the traditional Japanese tea ceremony as well as a number of lavish costumes which once graced the stage during performances of Noh. But the museum's real highlight is considered to be the display of sections of a 12th-century illustrated scroll of one of Japan's most celebrated novels: *The Tale of Genji*. The pieces are too fragile to be kept on permanent display, but

Osu Kannon Temple

Nagoya Festival

Nakagawa

Yabaton

all are exquisitely produced. History buffs might also like to take in a brief tour of the Shirakabe, Chikara and Shumoku-cho districts close to the museum, each of which offers a unique insight into 16th and 17th century life, when the roads were lined with homes belonging to the country's most famous warrior class: the *samurai*.

If your stomach calls following a tour on foot of Nagoya's historical sights, you could do worse than order up a specially-prepared plate of Nagoya *kochin*, locally-bred chicken famous throughout Japan for its succulent taste. A number of local restaurants prepare this dish in a variety of ways. One of the oldest and most respected in the business for its fresh chicken recipes is Nakagawa, located in Omatsu, no more than a five-minute walk from the Tokugawa Art Museum.

Shopping paradise in Osu

After lunch, jump on a bus and head across town to Nagoya's Osu district, a paradise for anyone keen to stroll through covered shopping arcades in search of a bargain. In the true spirit of ancient and modern, you'll find a choice of discount outlets selling the latest hi-tech electronic gadgets side-by-side with traditional Japanese sweet shops and clothing stores. Some of the best buys include televisions, cameras, laptop computers and stereo equipment of all shapes and sizes.

Osu is also the best place in the city to search for handcrafted Japanese antiques as well as used kimonos, which can often be snapped up for a fraction of the price of brand-new ones.

If you're in town at the right time, don't miss out on a trip to the flea market in the bustling precincts of the district's star attraction: the Osu Kannon temple. The market opens on the 18th and 28th of each month, but outside these times the lively temple is still an important local landmark which receives a steady, year-round stream of visitors. Worshippers flock here whatever the season, but the size of the crowd swells on public holidays or whenever a traditional festival is underway. One of the biggest is *Obon* (the festival of souls), which takes place in midsummer, but a number of smaller events are also held in the temple precincts at other times of the year.

If you're hungry for food rather than a bargain while shopping in Osu, take a seat at the counter inside Yabaton, a popular local restaurant which is something of an institution in Nagoya. Once you've made it to the front of the inevitable queue for a table, make sure you order the house speciality: *misokatsu*. The delicious, crispy breaded pork cutlets covered in thick, dark brown miso sauce are the perfect way to round off a day of fast-paced city sightseeing. Don't worry about the huge portions invariably offered up at Yabaton - the dish is not as heavy on the stomach as it looks!

A city that caters to all tastes and budgets

Hitting the streets of Nagoya in search of shops, restaurants and a place to unwind

Starting the day at the station

If Nagoya is at Japan's central crossroads, the actual point at which east and west meet is surely the area immediately surrounding Nagoya station. Far more than just a place to disembark from or board a bullet train, the city's transportation hub is an all-purpose meeting place packed with shops and restaurants. For a spectacular 360° panoramic view of the city and countryside beyond it, take the express elevator inside one of the two central towers to the 51st floor observation gallery. Look out on a clear day for the majestic peaks of the Japanese Alps which rise up in the distance.

If you can tear yourself away from the station complex, your first port of call should be the nearby Sakae district, a place where the city's major department stores and upscale shopping

Uiro

Temmusu

arcades converge. Dedicated shopaholics should head for Nadya Park, home to some of Nagoya's most fashionable boutiques. For a bird's eye view of the area as a whole, take a trip up Nagoya's 180m-high TV Tower, located within the open space of downtown Central Park. From here, it's hard to miss Oasis 21, the city's newest park located right in the heart of the Sakae district. Opened in October 2002, Oasis 21 is a futuristic model of urban space, a manmade paradise of water, trees, landscaped gardens and underground plazas, which collectively offer temporary respite from the noise of the city which surrounds it.

Bright lights in the all-night city

After dark, neon-lit Sakae becomes central Japan's equivalent of the Big Apple, the city which never sleeps, the place to see and to be seen. Night and day, you're never far from a place to eat in Sakae, but if you're too busy to spend time inside a restaurant, two local speciality snacks make for an ideal takeaway. Tasty bite-size rice balls filled with fried shrimp - known as *temmusu* - are the perfect fast food accompaniment to a can of hot green tea, which will help to wash down another local speciality: steamed cakes made with rice and sugar known as *uiro*. Available in a variety of flavours, the cakes can be eaten on the spot or packaged up and taken home as an edible souvenir of a trip around Aichi.

Winter can be cold in central Japan, and there's no better way to keep warm when the temperature drops than by tucking into a bowl of steaming hot noodles. As the fourth largest city in the country, Nagoya has its own speciality noodle dish known as *kishimen*, and noodle stands which serve it are to be found on the platforms of many railway stations in the region. Don't be afraid about formality while eating this particular dish. Slurping the noodles is supposed to improve the flavour and is actively encouraged.

JR Central Towers

Food Note: Kishimen

A popular speciality of Nagoya, *kishimen* are broad, flat, wheat noodles similar in texture to fettuccini. Cooked so they stay a little chewy, *kishimen* noodles are served in a soup flavoured with bonito stock and soy sauce. To prepare this popular winter dish, boil the noodles in water, drain and pour them into a bowl before adding the soup. as well as a dash of soy sauce. Deep-fried tofu bean curd and vegetables such as green onions or grated *daikon* radish are added later. Other ingredients commonly include egg or *tempura* (fish such as prawns deep-fried in batter).Top the entire dish off with a sprinkling of ground chilli pepper.

Going off the beaten track in search of Aichi's heritage

Shrines, gardens and traditional crafts are as much a part of life in Aichi as enterprise and manufacturing

Shirotori Garden

Tracking down an old neighbourhood

There's no need to go far in Nagoya to escape the frenetic pace of city life. A short train ride will bring you to Atsuta, an old neighbourhood that flourished during the Edo period and which is home to Atsuta Shrine, founded in the second century and widely regarded as the spiritual centre of the city. One of the three major Shinto shrines in Japan, the Atsuta complex is a peaceful haven set amid extensive grounds and surrounded by 1,000-year-old camphor trees. Housed within the shrine itself is the *Kusanagi-no-Mitsurugi* (grass-mowing sword), believed to be one of the three Sacred Treasures of the Imperial Family. Try to time your visit to coincide with one of the numerous colourful festivals and religious ceremonies held here each year. At weekends, the Noh theatre inside the shrine complex, more often than not comes alive with performances of Japan's ancient dramatic art.

Atsuta Shrine

A short walk from the shrine entrance brings you to another tranquil oasis, Shirotori Garden. The largest Japanese garden of its kind in Nagoya, Shirotori may lie a little off the beaten track, but the unusual combination of traditional and modern landscaping makes the journey worth the effort. The landscaped garden offers visitors a chance to escape the city streets and wander instead along pathways which wind around an interconnecting network of rivers and streams. The garden's theme is water, and inside you'll find a miniature version of central Japan's Kiso River - one of the cleanest and least polluted in the country - and even an artificial beach which replicates the ebb and flow of nearby Ise Bay. Adjacent to the strikingly modern Nagoya Congress Centre, Shirotori is a haven for busy conference delegates in search of fresh air, as well as members of the public looking for peace and quiet without having to stray far from the city centre.

Travelling to a place where time stands still

Just 20 minutes further along the railway line from Atsuta lies the town of Arimatsu, a place where time has stood still like almost nowhere else in Aichi, where rows of traditional wooden houses have been carefully preserved since the Edo period. Located along the old Tokaido Highway linking Kyoto with present-day Tokyo, Arimatsu is best-known as a centre for the traditional practice of tie-dyeing, known in Japan as *shibori*. The town has a 400-year history of tie-dyeing kimono fabric. Several centuries before the arrival of the bullet train, travellers embarking on the long journey by foot along the highway would stop in Arimatsu to rest, stock up on provisions and purchase tie-dyed clothes and towels fashioned by hand. Though the pedestrian travellers have long since abandoned the highway footpath in favour of the railway, thousands of visitors still flock to Arimatsu each year to relive the past, while craftsmen and women continue to keep the *shibori* tradition alive by making and selling an ornate selection of Japanese kimono fabrics.

If you're in the Atsuta area and looking for a bite to eat, consider a lunchtime trip to Atsuta-Horai-ken Jingu-Minami-Mae restaurant, located close to the Atsuta shrine complex. One of the most popular regional specialities originated here, and today people travel from all over Japan to order a portion of Nagoya's famous *hitsumabushi*, grilled eel on a bowl of steamed rice. The eel served up here is cut in far thinner slices than elsewhere in Japan and can be eaten together with *negi* (sliced leeks), *nori* (dried seaweed) and *wasabi*

(green horseradish). Some customers even add a splash of Japanese tea to the dish for additional flavour before tucking in. The meal can be eaten all year round, but is especially popular in summer, when eel is supposed to increase your stamina by helping to reduce your body heat.

Hitsumabushi

Nagoya map

Illustrator: Yuka Yoshida

NAGOYA CONVENTION & VISITORS BUREAU   http://www.ncvb.or.jp/location/

Checking out the sights away from the big city

Aichi – a place where traditional ways of life are still preserved today deep in the countryside

Korankei Gorge

Step back in time in rural Asuke

Once you've done all the sights in the big city, step back in time by making the short trip to nearby Asuke, home to a vast, open-air museum of traditional thatched houses which collectively offer the visitor an insight into how rural life was once led. Also not to be missed is Korankei Gorge, a vast wooded area which – courtesy of some 4,000 maples trees - is transformed during the autumn months into a sea of red and gold foliage. Get here as early as possible to beat the crowds. Spring is also busy here, when thousands descend on this river valley in the countryside outside Nagoya in time for the annual cherry blossom viewing season.

For many Japanese, traditional Aichi is synonymous with ceramics, and still today it's the hum of the potter's wheel which attracts visitors to make the short journey northeast from Nagoya to Seto, a picturesque town in the rolling hills of central Japan surrounded to the north and east by valleys covered in lush forest. Seto began to establish its reputation as one of the country's foremost centres for the production

of ceramics in the 12th to 14th centuries, and today the city remains as popular as ever with people looking for everything from handcrafted vases with million-dollar price tags to more everyday items such as rice bowls and tea cups. Bargain hunters should head here in time for the Setomono Festival on the second weekend of September, which is when street vendors lay out their wares and put them on sale at reduced prices. If you prefer to sightsee rather than shop, head instead for the Path of Kamagaki, a street lined with fences constructed entirely from tiny pieces of locally-produced ceramic – a quick stroll here is proof enough that Seto is itself a living museum of ceramics.

Tracking down Toyota's automobiles

An alternative daytrip from Nagoya with an altogether different pace can be made to the city of Toyota, home to the world-famous car manufacturer which bears the same name. Automobile fans might be tempted to combine a walk along the crystal-clear water of the city's Yahagi River with a trip to Toyota's exhibition hall, though the larger Toyota Automobile Museum in nearby Nagakute is also worth a visit. Vintage car enthusiasts will need plenty of time to take in the museum's vast collection of yesteryear vehicles spread across three floors – all are kept in mint condition. The second floor of the main exhibition building displays a selection of European and American vehicles, including a perfectly preserved 1910 Rolls Royce Silver Ghost and a shiny 1912 Cadillac from the United States. An equally impressive selection of Japanese cars – the oldest of which dates back to 1935 – is located on the third floor.

The view from above: thousands of people are expected to flock to the World Expo site in 2005

Nagakute may be home to Toyota's Automobile Museum, but it is also well-known as the site in 1584 of a fierce and bloody battle between two rival leaders, Tokugawa Ieyasu and Toyotomi Hideyoshi. Over four centuries on, Nagakute is today preparing to welcome the world as it gears up to host the 2005 World Exposition. For six months, the town will play host to the first truly international exhibition of the new century. As the countdown to the global event continues, the race is on to finish construction of Central Japan International Airport, scheduled to open for business in 2005 on an offshore island about 45km south of the Expo site.

Work has also already begun on a new, high-speed rail service which will connect Tokyo and Osaka via Nagoya. Once completed, the Linear Chuo Shinkansen – a new generation, magnetically-levitating train for the 21st century - will shuttle travellers at speeds of up to 500km per hour and reduce the journey time between the two cities to just 60 minutes. Billed as a lightning-fast, eco-friendly mode of transport for the future, the superconductive Maglev train has already undergone a successful series of test runs and is well on the way to becoming reality.

If you can't wait until 2005 to see the world on display in Nagakute, take a 30-minute side trip by rail from Nagoya to the castle town of Inuyama, where the Little World Museum of Man boasts a global collection of some 40,000 ethnic materials as well as 33 traditional houses from 22 countries. For an alternative view of Meiji-era Japan, Inuyama's open-air Meiji Mura Museum displays a variety of buildings which date back to the late 19th century, a period which saw the country finally abandon its long period of isolation from the rest of the world. Highlights include an 1898 telephone exchange which once stood in the northern city of Sapporo and a real, working steam locomotive which chugs the short distance between two stations named 'Tokyo' and 'Nagoya'.

One sight which is impossible to miss in Inuyama is the 450-year-old castle, perched on a hill overlooking the Kiso River. Built in 1537, it was partly destroyed during a devastating earthquake in 1891. Work to rebuild the castle was finally completed towards the end of the 1960s, and the donjon has now been restored to its former glory.

Path of Kamagaki

Toyota's Exhibition Hall
http://www.toyota.co.jp/company/factory/index2.html

Linear Chuo Shinkansen

Meiji Mura Museum

A prosperous castle town with a long history

Gifu City – culturally rich and geographically diverse

Gifu Wagasa (Japanese umbrellas)

Sweeping views from the castle on a hill

For centuries a prosperous castle town, the city of Gifu makes for an easy and convenient daytrip from the city of Nagoya. Your first stop – if only to get your bearings and to take in the breathtaking views of the surrounding area – should be Gifu Castle, perched on the top of Mt Kinka, which at 329m overlooks the Nagara River and is accessed via a ropeway from Gifu Park. The building which stands today on the site of the original castle is a 1956 reconstruction, but is still a foreboding and impressive fortification. On a clear day, take advantage of the aerial journey to the castle. There are excellent views of the city and the river which runs through it from inside the ropeway cabin. Information panels inside the castle trace the building's history, and there's a splendid photographic exhibition of dozens of other castles scattered around the country. Before heading back down towards the

city centre, look out for the audio-visual display inside the castle which introduces visitors to one of Gifu's most celebrated and ancient rituals: cormorant fishing.

From May to October, the Nagara River becomes a mecca for tourists who descend on Gifu from far and wide to witness the 1,300-year-old sight of fishermen dressed in traditional costume of straw skirt, sandals and black kimono using cormorant birds to fish at night for *ayu* (sweetfish). The birds, tied to reins and steered by fishermen standing inside the boats, dive down and catch the fish in their beaks. The rein around each bird's neck prevents it from swallowing any of the catch. It's a little-known fact that one of the film world's greatest comic heroes, Charlie Chaplin, took great delight in observing the art of cormorant fishing and visited Gifu on two separate occasions to see the fishermen and birds in action. For a modest fee, seats inside the boats are available to spectators who want to see the fishermen at work close-up. But there's no charge to stand along the river bank and witness the extraordinary night time spectacle of a river lit by fire and hundreds of cormorants diving into the water in search of a catch.

Souvenir hunters passing through Gifu City need look no further than the many shops selling paper lanterns and umbrellas, which have been produced in this area since at least the middle of the 18th century. Each part of the fragile but beautifully decorated objects is stitched together by hand using bamboo and high-quality paper.

Cormorant fishing

Food Note: Mitarashi Dango

A speciality of Gifu, *mitarashi* dango are grilled rice balls roasted on skewers and dipped in a soy sauce. The dumplings are made by mixing sticky rice flour with water and shaping the dough into marble-sized balls. They are then cooked on a grill until lightly browned on all sides before being generously brushed with a coating of freshly-prepared soy sauce. A popular sweet variety of the *mitarashi* sauce is made with soy and raw sugar, cooked together until the mixture thickens. Five of the balls are usually served on individual wooden skewers and dipped in the sauce before eating.

Heading into the mountains in search of the past

A tour of Takayama
- the town where time has stood still

Takayama Festival

Shirakawago

Wooden buildings and narrow streets

Located deep in the mountains of central Japan, in the region known traditionally as Hida, Takayama is deservedly one of the most popular destinations in the country, combining as it does ancient traditions with a stunning natural location. Often referred to as 'little Kyoto', the old streets of Takayama are lined with temples, shrines, small museums, traditional shops and inns. The greatest pleasure comes from the chance to wander round the old, narrow lanes of wooden houses, investigate the fruit and vegetable stalls at the daily morning markets and hunt around for souvenirs such as lacquer ware, wood craft and pottery.

The town is at its busiest during the spring and autumn festivals, when 300,000 people come to see huge, 300-year-old, ornately-decorated floats paraded through the streets. Outside of the festival seasons, several of the large floats are put on display at the Float Exhibition Hall in the centre of town.

An early evening dip in a hot spring is considered by many to be the ideal way of rounding off a day of frenetic sightseeing in Japan. If you're in search of a hot tub, try the Okuhida Spa Resort at the western foot of the Japanese Alps. The collective name for a group of five individual spas, Okuhida is most famous for its *rotenburo*, outdoor baths which offer visitors the opportunity to soak away aches and pains while taking in the views of snow-capped peaks stretching into the distance.

Don't wind up a tour of the region without including a stop in the mountain village of Shirakawago. This UNESCO World Heritage site in northwest Gifu is home to over 100 traditional gassho-style farmhouses with steep thatched roofs, a centuries-old design to protect each home – and its occupants – from the heavy winter snowfall.

The mountainous region of northern Gifu is fertile territory for magnolia trees, the leaves of which are used in *hoba miso*, a Takayama speciality of *miso* mixed with vegetables and roasted on a magnolia leaf. Once a popular dish with woodcutters who used to cook *miso* on top of heated rocks deep in the forest, the speciality is often accompanied with *saké* from one of Takayama's own breweries. Plenty of restaurants serve *hoba miso* as a house speciality, but if you're up for the culinary challenge of doing it yourself, most of the souvenir shops in town offer a kit that includes a tiny, candle-powered grill, magnolia leaves and *miso*.

Okuhida Spa Resort

Food Note: Hoba miso

Hoba miso is a traditional Takayama speciality of *miso* (fermented soybean paste) mixed with a variety of seasonal vegetables and cooked on a magnolia leaf. The vegetables – anything from chopped *shiitake* mushrooms to green onions, shallots or leeks - are mixed with lightly-seasoned *miso* before being placed on a large, sun-dried magnolia leaf, and roasted over an open flame. Often cooked directly at restaurant tables, this dish can be served with rice and a selection of pickles and should be eaten piping hot. *Hoba miso* is usually enjoyed either as a snack with *saké* or as a side dish.

The 'Michi' Interview

'Michi' is the Japanese word for 'Way'
meaning path of self refinement.

Macrobiotics
Michio Kushi

As a pioneer of world peace through macrobiotics, Michio Kushi's work spans over 50 years. Macrobiotics is the art and science of health and longevity. It seeks to understand the interaction between ourselves and the foods we eat, the lifestyle we choose and the environment in which we live. A macrobiotic diet consists of whole, natural foods and is primarily made up of grains such as brown rice or millet, a variety of locally grown vegetables and beans. Macrobiotics has attracted famous followers such as Gwyneth Paltrow, Madonna and Tom Cruise.

Michio Kushi has advised numerous government leaders and organisations including the United Nations and the World Health Organisation, and has testified at the White House Commission on Complementary and Alternative Medicine. In 1998 the National Museum of American History (Smithsonian Institute) acquired the collected works of Mr Kushi and his wife Aveline in recognition of the major part they have played in the shift towards healthier eating habits in America. The author of several dozen books, Mr Kushi continues to oversee all programmes offered by the Kushi Institute.

Interviewers: Anna Thomson / Fumiaki Tanaka   Photographer: Joji Sawa

With a better understanding of food and the environment I'd encourage humankind to develop peacefully and spiritually...that is my dream.

We visited Mr Kushi at the international headquarters of the Kushi Institute nestling in the heart of the Berkshire Mountains in Massachusetts. We were fortunate to be invited to a celebratory meal on New Year's Day prepared by Mr Kushi himself. Prolonged snowstorms delayed our departure and due to his busy schedule the interview was postponed several times. However, this gave us the opportunity to slow down and acquire a deeper understanding of the man and his work. Dressed in his customary three-piece-suit and adopting a slow but charismatic manner, Mr Kushi spoke at length about his philosophy and how he emerged from war torn Japan to become one of the most prolific leaders in America's natural health movement.

Can you tell us a little about your childhood and youth?

I was born on 17 May 1926 in Wakayama in central Japan. My parents were both teachers and I moved around a lot in my childhood. When I was 12 years old the war between Japan and China started, and when I was 16 Japan entered World War Two. Whilst studying at Tokyo University large areas of the city were destroyed by B-29s and food became more and more scarce. As the war intensified I was drafted to go to the southern islands of Okinawa. Half of my classmates died when the boat sank on the way. I remained in Kyushu and was stationed at Tosu station an hour away from Nagasaki.

On 6 August 1945 all communication suddenly stopped from Hiroshima. There was a lot of speculation. Later we realised that Hiroshima had been completely destroyed, then three days later Nagasaki was bombed. We helped many of the injured people who were transported out of Nagasaki by train.

How did you change from soldier to world peace activist?

Like all young people at that time I didn't care about dying, but after the war ended I realised I had to continue to live. Whilst studying at graduate school, I came to realise the need for a world federation so that war would never happen again. I began corresponding with America's United World Federalists. They advised me that there was a World Government Association in Tokyo. I visited there and met my teacher George Ohsawa (b. 1893). He didn't talk about political science but about philosophy, life and Yin and Yang. I came to America in 1949 to attend a World Federation Convention. At that time, very few people could get out of Japan. Fortunately one of the World Federalists, Norman Cousins, acted as my guarantor. I was encouraged to stay and enter Colombia University and there I started to gather the ideas of various people from Plato to Thomas Mann, who envisioned a harmonious world order.

When I was 25 I started to think that even if a world government were created, unless human nature became truly peaceful it would not be a way to secure harmony. Otherwise we would still need strict laws, the army and police and that is not a true peace. Instead we need to develop a more peaceful and loving human nature. It's very easy to talk about brotherhood and peace, but that kind of human nature must come naturally, from inside. I wanted to ask the guidance of my senior World Federalists and visited Dr. Einstein, Norman Cousins, Thomas Mann, and many others. But their answers were: 'We don't know, we don't know how to make human nature peaceful'. They said, 'Only you yourself must understand.'

And you found the answer in food?

Yes, I questioned whether I should continue to study political science. I wanted to know what humanity is and how human beings can become peaceful, so I decided to give up my studies. I stood in Times Square every day. Morning till night, I watched thousands and thousands of people. Every day. Everyone was different. Some were walking fast, some were walking slow, some were tall, some small, some were blond and some brunette. I questioned why we have two eyes, two ears and one nose. Why? Why do we have thoughts, what is intuition and imagination? What is memory? I wondered about all these things as I watched people go by.... Then, (snaps his fingers) a flash came. All beings, not only humans, but also animals and plants, we are all governed and influenced by our environment, seasonal changes and cosmic forces. I thought that if there were some factors that we could control then we could change ourselves. So I started to consider them and one by one I cancelled out those we can't control - sunshine, air and so on until one remained. That was food. Food we are able to control 100%. I started to think I have to change America by food, as it was the leading force of the world. Unless we change America we will not have peace.

Could you explain further about how food can affect our thoughts and actions?

Food is not only for sustaining the body. Food changes into vibrations through digestion. Energy and calories are all vibrations that change our way of thinking. Thoughts are vibrations. So a certain way of eating will make us more competitive, materialistic or aggressive and other ways will make us more peaceful and spiritual, especially if this is continued over generations. Following a macrobiotic diet, the mind becomes peaceful, so I never become angry or jealous.

So how did macrobiotics start?

Actually, basic macrobiotic principles have been known to philosophers and physicians throughout history. Its present form evolved from the ideas of Sagen Ishizuka (b. 1851) an army doctor who formed a dietary theory using foods to heal illness. He adopted both western medicine and eastern traditions. When my teacher George Ohsawa was young he got TB. After reading Ishizuka's book *Shoku You* (Food Nourishment) he began to practise the diet and cured himself. Ohsawa became a disciple of Ishizuka and extended the theory. He incorporated the concept of Yin and Yang and gave it the name 'Macrobiotics', which comes from Greek and means longevity. My wife Aveline was a student of George Ohsawa in Tokyo. She arrived in America about two and half years after me. With her, I formulated my ideas to establish standard macrobiotics.

Can you explain more about Yin and Yang?

Every phenomenon is constantly changing between two antagonistic or complementary tendencies; expansion and contraction, upward and downward, the earthly ascending force and the heavenly descending force. All of these are comprehensively called Yin and Yang and form the foundation

Even if a world government were created, unless human nature became truly peaceful it would not be a way to secure harmony. It's very easy to talk about brotherhood and peace, but that kind of human nature must come naturally, from inside.

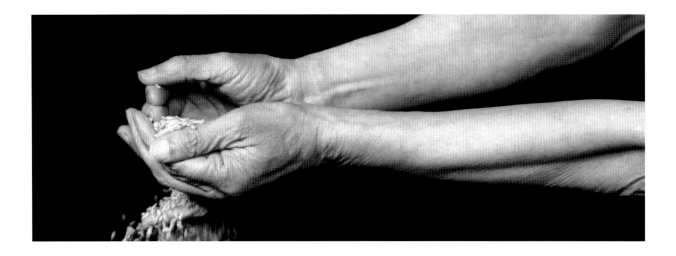

Hippies were anti-system. They wanted to have a new world and my lectures and writings fitted into their philosophy.

of oriental philosophies. In ancient times political leaders, thinkers and doctors would have studied this otherwise they would not be able to understand life. All Oriental traditions, from flower arranging to Aikido, are based on this idea. It also applies to food. Yin type foods like fruit or greens have an earth expanding force. Yang type foods such as root vegetables like carrots or burdock have the heaven's force, which is more contracting. We must have a good balance of foods in our diet.

Does macrobiotics forbid the consumption of meat?

Evolutionally, mammals are very near to us whereas fish are further away. So if you would like to eat animal products a small portion of fish is better. Macrobiotics is not a rigid framework but what is really necessary for that person, each individual has the freedom to choose. Macrobiotics offers guidelines, but within that you can eat meat sometimes. However you should know that while eating meat your spiritual quality is hindered.

Why and how did so many hippies come to study with you in the 60's?

At that time I was lecturing in New York, but in order to really influence America I needed to move to Boston, the intellectual centre of America. We anticipated maybe students of Harvard would come but instead some hippies came from San Francisco. Then they started to call their friends. Around 1960 several hundred hippies had gathered in Boston. Hippies were anti-system. They wanted to have a new world and my lectures and writings fitted into their philosophy. Then, we set up a study house and I taught shiatsu massage and my wife Aveline, also taught cooking. That's how it all began. Many people took drugs like marijuana, and LSD. In order to stop that, we said the brown rice and miso soup would make you higher. I was suspected by the city authorities to be the boss of a drug movement, and so I was literally followed by the police. Mu tea, a macrobiotic drink made from nine kinds of herbs, was suspected and analysed for drugs. (Laughs) Now it's funny but at the time it was very serious.

Can you tell me something about your consultancy work with the major Japanese convenience store chain Lawson?

I gave a lecture about how the quality of our diet has changed in the 20th Century to the president and directors at the headquarters of Lawson in Tokyo. I told them, 'I visited three Lawson stores and there was nothing that I wanted to buy'. I thought I would upset them but instead they all nodded. After

that about 10 people, including the president, came to see me individually for personal health consultations. This directed some staff towards the idea of eating for health. Later they came up with the idea of a separate subsidiary, Natural Lawson, and asked for my guidance. A pilot store opened in Tokyo in 2002, and they became popular. Unfortunately, it is not all organic yet but within the price range they did their best. Two months ago I heard they have four stores.

You mention that it is important to do what you love. Can you give us some advice?

Don't sell your life! I am always saying this in my lectures. Today, from kindergarten it's always education, education, education, and competition. The reason is to sell your life at a higher price. And then you start work in an enterprise or in government and then it becomes all about position and higher income. Every day, how much; every week, how much; every month, how much - you are selling your life, like slicing off *kamaboko* fish cake. Every year, you hope to sell at a higher price. Then, at nearly sixty, you start to worry because the piece is becoming smaller and smaller. Finally only a bit remains but no one buys, so you retire …and then die. Meanwhile you have sold ALL your life.
Instead, don't sell your life, do whatever you really want to do. You must act as the master of your life, and then you become free. However difficult it is, however unsuccessful it seems, do whatever you want!

What is your aim for the future?

Continue this dream! First, with a better understanding of food and the environment I'd encourage humankind to develop peacefully and spiritually. Second, change the economic and industrial systems to using new technologies that don't pollute. Third, create a world government and fourth, I'd like a spiritual human race to develop from homo sapiens to homo pacifica and further develop into homo spiritual and this spiritual civilisation will populate this entire earth. That is my dream and beyond that it's your dream!

What does *michi*, the way, mean to you?

My name! (Laughs) Also it is the way of the universe, or Yin and Yang. For human beings *michi* means interpret and act that way. However conceptually, just to think I should do this or that is no good. Instead actions and thoughts should come naturally. For that, again, we must eat well. In a healthy person, natural actions arise. That is *michi*.

Japanese Food Glossary

日本食材図鑑

Kome (Hakumai)
Japonica Rice

Hakumai (white rice) generally refers to polished short-grain Japonica rice and is a highly nutritious source of protein, fibre, Vitamin B, calcium and iron. A staple of the Japanese diet since ancient times, *hakumai* is also an excellent source of energy, and forms part of the traditional Japanese meal combination along with *miso* soup, and *tsukemono*. As well as being easier to digest than *genmai*, *hakumai*'s glutinous texture means that it is easier to pick up with chopsticks and its mild taste makes it a perfect accompaniment to almost any food.

Genmai
Japonica Brown Rice

Genmai is unpolished brown rice with the husks removed but the bran and germ intact. Slightly nutty tasting and more 'chewy' than *hakumai*, *genmai* is both delicious and extremely nutritious, containing four times the Vitamin B1 and E, three times the fibre, and twice the Vitamin B2 and iron of *hakumai*. Good with almost any ingredient, *genmai* can be used as a substitute for *hakumai* and can also be made into a wonderful rice porridge. Since it contains an element that naturally stimulates the metabolism, it assists in reducing the signs of aging, and improves the condition of hair and skin.

Mochigome/Mochi
Glutinous Rice/Rice Cake

Mochigome is a variety of rice with a slightly sweet flavour and a high starch content. It is pounded in a tub until it becomes extremely sticky, and then formed into small squares or round *mochi* (rice cake). *Mochi* is traditionally grilled and wrapped in *nori*, or cooked in soup. One such soup is *zouni* (a soup dish with *mochi* and vegetables), which is eaten to celebrate New Year. There are many different variations of this soup throughout Japan. The stickiness of the *mochi* represents the idea of 'sticking to your principles', making it a good omen for the start of a new year.

Nuka
Rice Bran

Nuka is made during the process of polishing *genmai,*. and is most commonly used to make *tsukemono*. It contains protein, fibre, calcium, phosphorous, iron and Vitamins A, B1 and B2. Its alkaline quality is effective in the regeneration of new, smooth skin, making it an excellent beauty product. The fibre content can help remove cancer-causing elements by discharging toxins from the body. It is beneficial in treating diabetes, reducing blood cholesterol rates and preventing sclerosis of the arteries.

Sake
Rice Wine

Sake, Japan's national alcoholic drink, is made from fermented rice. Brown rice is 'polished' to make the smaller white rice grains used in the brewing of *sake*, which is categorized according to the the degree of rice polishing: *junmaishu* (pure rice *sake*), *honjozo* (*sake* with a limited addition of brewer's alcohol), *ginjoshu* (the highest grade category) and *futsushu* (common grades of *sake*). *Sake* is clear, but sometimes has a yellow tint. It has a slightly sweet taste and an alcohol content of 14 to 16%. Traditionally, it is served warm in a small porcelain cup or cold in a glass.

Biru
Japanese Beer

Beer was first test-brewed in Japan in 1853, following a Dutch recipe. The country's first brewery was established in the 1870's and since then, beer, especially lager, has become very popular as an accompaniment to Japanese food. Japanese beer drinkers consider how well a beer refreshes the throat and cleans the palate as being particularly important (an aspect known as '*kire*' – literally, 'cutting'), and major Japanese beers are especially brewed for a sharp, clean finish. In 1994, the minimum production quantity needed for a brewery to obtain a manufacturing licence was reduced, and since then many small regional breweries have been established, providing a great variety of original beers.

Uisuki

Whisky

Using the same ingredients and methods as in the West, Japanese whisky is made to accompany Japanese-style meals. Particular importance is attached to the harmonized balance of a steady foundation of flavour, which is not broken down when diluted by water, and a subtlety of taste well suited to the Japanese palate that does not diminish the delicate flavours of Japanese food. This feature is well accepted in Japan, where the cultural background makes it ideal for whisky to be drunk with the meal, instead of after it, as in Western countries. As a result, Japanese whisky goes well with food, while Scotch whisky, with its representative smoky flavour and strong peat taste, is better on its own.

Shochu

Japanese Clear Spirit

Made from a variety of ingredients such as wheat, sweet potato and corn, *shochu* is distinguished from Western spirits by the use of *koji*, (a 'starter' used in the making of *sake*, soy sauce, and *miso*) at the stage of initial fermentation. Depending on the distillation method used, *shochu* is divided into two categories: the single distillation method is used to make traditional *shochu*, in which more of the flavour of its ingredients is retained. The multiple distillation method is well suited for making cocktails and fruit liquors. *Shochu* contains no fat or sugar, and is good drunk with hot water, in cocktails, or on its own.

Umeshu

Plum Wine

Umeshu, with its subtle sweet flavour, has been consumed for over 1,000 years in Japan. This wine is made from green ume plums, *shochu* and sugar, and is left to mature for between three months and one year. Because of the healthy properties of *ume*, *umeshu* is popular not only as an aperitif and for drinking with meals, but also as a medicine. *Ume* plums are rich in minerals such as potassium and calcium and contain large amounts of fruit acid, which aids digestion and breaks down lactic acid. They are also said to increase the body's metabolic rate and reduce tiredness.

ALCOHOLIC DRINKS
TEAS

Ryokucha

Green Tea

Ryokucha is produced from leaves that are steamed and dried but not fermented. The quality of *ryokucha* varies according to which part of the plant is picked, such as *gyokuro* (high quality *ryokucha*) and *sencha* (middle quality *ryokucha*). The leaves produce a greenish-yellow tea and a flavour that is slightly bitter and closer to the taste of the fresh leaf. The tannin in *ryokucha* serves as a disinfectant against tooth decay. It also contains caffeine and Vitamin C. It is said to be effective against diabetes, high blood pressure and in reducing cholesterol levels.

Hojicha/Genmaicha

Toasted Tea/Brown Rice Tea

Variants of *ryokucha*, *hojicha* is made by roasting *bancha* (coarse tea) or *sencha* (middle quality *ryokucha*), creating a strong toasted aroma. *Genmaicha* is also a variation of *bancha* and *sencha*. It is a mixture of either of these teas with fried grains of rice. Unlike *ryokucha*, boiling water is used to make both *hojicha* and *genmaicha*. This helps to bring out the pleasant bitterness of tannin and imparts a little sweetness. All types of tea should be stored in a cool place, and it is best drunk while its fresh taste and flavour are maintained.

Mugicha

Barley Tea

Made from roasted barley, *mugicha* has a clear, dark brown colour and does not contain caffeine or tannin. Recent findings show that *mugicha* has anti-oxidant qualities that act against aging and illnesses such as cancer and diabetes. It can be served hot, but cold *mugicha* is particularly good to quench your thirst in summer. Cold *mugicha* can be made simply by steeping tea bags in cold water. However, it is at its best when boiled for at least five minutes and then cooled.

Shoyu

Soy Sauce

This oriental sauce is very popular all over the world and is used to add flavour to a wide range of dishes, both in cooking and at the table. Made from soy beans, wheat and salt, and fermented for six to eight months, Japanese soy sauce has a rich aroma, a salty, yet subtle and complex flavour and comes in several varieties. *Koikuchi shoyu*, developed in the east of Japan, has a dark colour and slightly fruity flavour that reduces the fishy and meaty smells of certain dishes. *Usukuchi shoyu*, originally favoured in the west of Japan, has a lighter colour and saltier taste than *koikuchi*.

Miso

Fermented Soy Bean Paste

There's an old Japanese saying: "a bowl of *miso* soup a day keeps the doctor away", and many Japanese follow this advice. *Miso* is made from soy beans and usually rice or barley, which are steamed, mixed with *koji* (a starter) and left to ferment for six months to five years. There are three types of *miso*: red, white and medium - the longer the fermentation, the darker the *miso*. Modern analysis shows that this salty and flavoursome paste is an extremely nourishing and well-balanced food containing protein, vitamins and essential amino acids. As well as being great for soups, it is used to add flavour to many dishes.

Tofu

Soy Bean Curd

Tofu is eaten cooked or fresh with a sauce and is delicious in dishes such as *miso* soup, hot-pots and stir-fries. Made from ground soy beans, which are heated, filtered, and, with the addition of a gelling agent, hardened into evenly sized squares. *Tofu* comes in three basic types: *kinugoshi-dofu* (silk strained *tofu*), the original Japanese *tofu*, fine textured and eaten raw; *momen-dofu* (cotton strained *tofu*), which is rougher in texture; and *yose-dofu* (crumbled *tofu*): which is not formed into blocks and appears as though mashed. *Tofu* is an extremely nutritious food containing plenty of easy-to-digest vegetable protein, calcium, iron and Vitamin E.

Abura Age

Fried Bean Curd

Momen-dofu style *tofu* is thinly sliced and fried in oil first at 110-120°C until it swells fully, and then at 180-200°C. This process of double frying enables the inside to retain the texture of *tofu* while the outer skin keeps the moisture out and stays crisp. It is placed on top of *kitsune udon* ('fox' *udon* noodles), which is in accordance with an old tale that says that the sly fox put a piece of *abura age* on his head just before he disappeared. It is also used to make *inari zushi* (sweetened and cooked *abura age* filled with *sushi* rice).

Tofu Seihin

Tofu Products

Tofu's mild taste makes it a very versatile food that can be used to make many different products. *Koyadofu* is named after a temple on Koya Mountain, where it is said to have originated from. *Tofu* is quickly frozen at below -15°C, enabling the preservation of all the nutritious value of the *tofu*. *Koyadofu* is also referred to as *koridofu* (frozen *tofu*) because of this freezing method. *Ganmodoki* is a fried tofu dumpling often made with vegetables and sesame seeds. *Atsuage* is the name for strips of *tofu* that are deep-fried just once.

Natto

Fermented Soy Beans

Natto is made from fermented soy beans and has a sticky consistency and a strong characteristic 'fermented' smell that, like certain strong cheeses, some might find unpleasant. An excellent source of protein, Vitamin B2, iron and fibre, *natto* is often mixed with soy sauce and other ingredients and eaten with boiled rice as a traditional and nutritious breakfast food. Apart from the standard whole bean variety, *natto* also comes in small-bean and chopped-bean forms. It contains an amino acid not found in other foods that helps prevent blood clots, which can cause strokes and coronaries.

Daizu/Azuki

Soy Beans/Red Beans

Beans are a rich source of Vitamin B1, protein, calcium and fibre. They can be used whole, fresh or dried, or in processed form. *Daizu* (soy beans) contain less fat than meat yet plenty of low-calorie protein which make them an excellent choice for vegetarians. *Edamame*, a less mature form of *daizu*, are green beans in their pod and are often eaten boiled and salted as a snack with beer or other alcoholic drinks. This is quite a wise practice as the amino acid in their protein helps to break down the alcohol in the body and thus reduces hangovers. *Azuki* are sweet-tasting red beans which are most often used to make sweets in Japan.

Anko

Red Bean Paste

Anko is made from *azuki* and sugar, and is used in traditional Japanese confectionery. The two main types of *anko* are *tsubu-an* (*anko* made from a lightly mashed paste so that beans retain their shape) and *koshi-an* (smooth, thoroughly blended *anko*). *Azuki* is a well-balanced nutritious food source; it contains linolenic acid, which helps to lower cholesterol, anti-aging Vitamin E, protein and calcium. Some people fear that *anko*'s sweetness makes it fattening, however, it is full of fibre and contains much less fat than confectionery made with cream.

Kinako

Parched Soy Bean Flour

Kinako is finely ground flour made from soy beans. The *ki-* in the name stems from the word *kiiro* (yellow), which suggests its light brownish-yellow colour. Its flavour is slightly nutty. *Kinako* contains twice the protein of wheat flour and is very low in carbohydrates. It is abundant in fibre, iron, calcium, vitamins and minerals, and is therefore very effective for many ailments such as high cholesterol. It is not eaten on its own, but mixed with other flours in cooking, and in confectionery, such as *kinako mochi* (rice cakes covered in *kinako*).

Harusame

Bean Noodles

Harusame are translucent, thin noodles, originally made in China from the starch of *ryoku-tou* (green mung beans). The Japanese adapted the main ingredient to create noodles from potato and sweet potato starch. This method became widespread during the post-war period and is now popular in Japan. *Harusame* are available in dried form and need to be soaked in water before using. These noodles have a naturally tender texture that suit a variety of dishes including soups and salads.

Goma

Sesame Seeds

Sesame seeds are a very popular Japanese seasoning and are used in a number of different ways. *Goma-shio* (mixed black sesame seeds and salt) is often used as an all-purpose seasoning. Another popular way of using sesame is in *goma-ae*, which is a dish of vegetables such as boiled spinach, sugarsnap peas or burdock mixed with a sesame sauce. High in Vitamin E, sesame seeds help to prevent the greying of hair and the skin becoming dry. As sesame seeds are half composed of unsaturated fatty acids, they help to reduce cholesterol levels. They are good for brittle bones, headaches, high blood pressure and arteriosclerosis.

Goma Abura

Sesame Oil

Sesame oil is used in stir-fries and fried dishes as well as for seasoning. With its delicious aroma and rich, nutty flavour, it plays an important role in defining the taste of Oriental food. Compared with other cooking oils, sesame oil does not easily become oxidised, which means linoleic acid and oreinate acids remain active, reducing 'bad' cholesterol. Sesame oil differs depending on whether it is extracted from toasted or fresh sesame seeds. If toasted seeds are used, the aroma of the oil is strong and it is dark brown in colour. If fresh seeds are used, the oil tastes richer and its colour lighter.

BEANS/SEEDS OILS

39

Komezu
Rice Vinegar

Made from rice, this light and mild tasting Japanese vinegar is an essential ingredient for making *sushi* rice and *sunomono* (vinegared salads). It has a lower acid level than Western vinegars and has long been associated with youthful-looking skin and longevity. One reason for this is the fact that vinegar increases the potency of Vitamin C, which promotes good complexion, and in the past, *komezu* was used in cosmetics in Japan. Vinegar is also known for its anti-bacterial properties and this is one reason why *komezu* is often used in Japanese dishes that include raw fish, seafood and meat.

Mirin
Sweet Cooking *Sake*

Mirin is made from distilled spirit, *koji* (a starter) and rice. It is one of Japan's principal condiments. It is sweet and syrupy, and has an alcohol content of about 13-14%, which is often burnt off during cooking. *Mirin* has a subtle, natural sweetness, and its balanced flavour makes it a very versatile condiment. *Mirin* is used to add sweetness to dishes such as *nimono* (simmered dishes), for marinating and glazing, and in *teriyaki* sauce. Along with soy sauce and *dashi*, it is known as one of the three essential tastes of old Japan.

Ryorishu
Cooking *Sake*

Sake is the premiere Japanese alcoholic drink but there is also a version made especially for cooking. *Ryorishu*, made from fermented rice, is often used in marinades for meat and fish to soften them as well as to mask their smell. In cooking, it is often used to add body and flavour to various *tsuyu* (soup stock) and sauces, or to make *nimono* (simmered dishes) and *yakimono* (grilled dishes). To enable non alcohol-licensed shops to store it, manufacturers are required by law to add salt (2-3%) cooking *sake* to make it unfit for drinking.

Funmatsu Dashi
Powdered Soup Stock

Dashi is the stock which forms the basis of almost all Japanese cooking. *Katsuobushi*, *konbu*, and *iriko* are the basic ingredients of *dashi*. The powdered variety is very popular for use as an instant soup stock. Based on one or a combination of the basic *dashi* ingredients, powdered *dashi* is mixed with other condiments according to the dish and individual taste. Although it is easy and quick to prepare, powdered *dashi* can be used to create authentic tasting Japanese cuisine and is a highly versatile product. It is used for flavouring dishes such as soups, hot pots, sauces, rice dishes and salad dressings.

Umami Chomiryo
Umami Seasoning

Umami (monosodium glutamate), a powerful flavour-enhancer derived from glutamic acid and one of the amino acids, was first discovered by Japanese scientists early in the 20th century. Found naturally in seaweed and vegetables, *umami* is one of the four elements that make up *umami chomiryo*, a flavour-enhancing product commonly known in Japan as *Ajinomoto*. Though *umami chomiryo* has no pronounced flavour or colour of its own, it brings out and complements the '*umami* factor' of food when sprinkled onto it. *Umami chomiryo* is used in the preparation of meat and fish, to season soups, in steamed and slow cooking dishes, in sauces and salad dressings.

Sosu
Sauce

Originating from Worcester sauce, Japanese '*sosu*' developed in a very unique way. As with other Western foods, Worcester sauce was adapted (using various kinds of vegetables, fruits and spices, and adding vinegar, salt and sugar) to suit Japanese tastes. It is generally used to season *yoshoku* (Japanese style Western dishes such as croquettes and cutlets). There are several types of Japanese 'sauce', 'Worcester sauce': a thin, spicy sauce based on its English namesake and often used as a 'secret ingredient'. *Tonkatsu* sauce is a thick sauce with a mild, sweet taste suitable for fried dishes. *Chuno* sauce has both a mild and spicy flavour suitable for stewed dishes.

Tare
Dipping Sauce

There are many dipping sauces used for Japanese grilled and pot dishes. *Yakiniku no tare* (barbecue sauce) is made from soy sauce, fruits, vegetables, sesame oil, and herbs and spices. It is used not only for dipping sauce but also to marinade meat before roasting. *Sukiyaki no tare*, a mildly sweet sauce, is made from soy sauce, *mirin*, sugar and *dashi*, and used to stew *sukiyaki* ingredients. *Shabu-shabu no tare*, a dipping sauce used for lightly cooked and thinly sliced meats, comes in several varieties such as *ponzu* sauce and *goma* sauce.

Ponzu
Citrus Vinegar

Ponzu is derived from the Dutch word 'pons', which means citrus juice. *Ponzu* is a mixture of *su* (vinegar), and citrus fruit juice (such as lemon, *sudachi*, *yuzu*, and *kabosu*). It has a refreshing taste, and just a few drops of *ponzu* adds something special to a great variety of dishes. It is also a good stimulant, since the acid found in *ponzu* breaks down fat and lactic acids, which cause fatigue. *Ponzu* is most commonly used as *ponzu-shoyu*; a dipping sauce for *nabe*. *Ponzu-shoyu* is made by mixing *ponzu*, *shoyu*, sugar or *mirin*, and *dashi*.

Doresshingu
Salad Dressing

The Japanese have created many new great tasting foods by adapting the foods of other nations. Japanese salad dressings are a particularly good example of this trend. Made from ingredients such as soy sauce, sesame oil and seeds, *shiso*, *umeboshi*, *yuzu* and *dashi*, these dressings perfectly complement salads containing Japanese ingredients such as *tofu*, seaweed, *konnyaku*, *daikon* radish and *sashimi*. There are also wonderful Japanese versions of classic Western dressings such as French, Thousand Islands, and Caesar.

SAUCES SPICES

Men-tsuyu
Soup for Noodles

Men-tsuyu, made from *dashi*, soy sauce, *mirin* and sugar, is an essential ingredient for *soba* and *udon* noodle dishes. There are two basic types of *men-tsuyu*: *kake-tsuyu*, which is poured hot over boiled noodles to make noodle soup, and *tsuke-tsuyu*, which literally means 'dipping soup' and is used as a dip for chilled noodles. Ready-made concentrated *men-tsuyu* is generally designed for both uses. *Kake-tsuyu* is diluted with hot water, whereas *tsuke-tsuyu* is used straight, or thinned with a little water.

Wasabi
Japanese Horseradish

Wasabi is a root plant with a pleasant aroma and a sharp, fiery flavour. In early 17th century Japan, it became a popular accompaniment to *sushi*, prompting the spread of its cultivation. *Wasabi* is available fresh, and can be grated like horseradish, as a paste or in powder form, which is mixed with lukewarm water to make a light green paste. It is also mixed with soy sauce and served as a condiment with *sashimi* and *sushi*. When used for seasoning, *wasabi* can stimulate the appetite and it is also known to prevent food poisoning.

Wagarashi
Japanese Mustard

Wagarashi is made from the seeds of the *karashina* plant, and in ancient times was used as a medicine as well as a food. Bright yellow in colour, *wagarashi* is available in both paste and powder forms, and is used to add spiciness and flavour to *natto*, *shumai* (Chinese dumplings), *oden* (kind of Japanese hot pot), and salad dressings. It does not include vinegar and the intensity of its flavour is greater than that of Western mustard. It is similar in quality to that of *wasabi*, therefore, *wagarashi* is usually used in very small quantities.

SPICES
SEAWEEDS

Shichimi/Ichimi Togarashi
Seven Spice Pepper/Chilli Pepper

Shichimi togarashi, which means 'seven-taste chilli pepper', is a dried mixture of red chilli flakes, *sansho*, *goma*, *nori*, dried mandarin or orange peel, hemp and poppy seeds. Popular throughout Japan, the ingredients and balance of these mixes vary from region to region. It is usually sprinkled on hot *udon* noodle soup and many other dishes to add flavour, spiciness and aroma. *Shichimi togarashi* is known to be a good remedy for colds and flu, and is also considered to be beneficial for the stomach. *Ichimi* means one taste. *Ichimi togarashi* consists of just Japanese chilli pepper.

Nori
Nori Seaweed

Nori, a dried seaweed resembling sheets of black paper, is a very popular ingredient in Japan, particularly for the wrapping of steamed rice to make *maki-zushi* (rolled *sushi*) and *onigiri* (rice balls). *Nori* is an ideal food for those whose lungs have been damaged by smoking as it can help prevent tar attaching itself to the lungs. It is also said to prevent anaemia, hair loss and greying. It is rich in vitamin B1, which helps combat mental fatigue, and calcium. Seasoned *nori* is also popular.

Yakumi
Other Japanese Spices

Japanese people have used spices as condiments, seasonings, medicines and aromatic enhancers in cooking since ancient times. *Shiso* seeds are used to add flavour to *shiozuke* (salted pickles) and *tsukudani*. *Myoga* is a native plant to Japan, and its peppery component can help improve blood circulation, and relieve sore throats. *Sansho* is an aromatic spice made from the dried ground pods of the prickly ash tree. Sometimes referred to as 'Japanese pepper', it is often used to counteract the greasiness of dishes such as grilled eel.

Wakame
Wakame Seaweed

This dark green seaweed with its light 'ocean' flavour is one of the most popular seaweeds in Japan. It is available in both dry and fresh forms and is most commonly used in soups and salads. The dried product greatly expands when it's reconstituted either by soaking in water for a few minutes or adding directly to a soup, so you often find that you need far less than you originally thought. Since *wakame* has no calories, it is an ideal ingredient for those who want to control their weight and is allegedly good for treating arteriosclerosis, asthma, sinusitis, goitre, high blood pressure and hair loss.

Konbu
Kelp

Konbu is the basic *dashi* ingredient. To make good stock, simply soak *konbu* in water, or heat in a pan of water on a medium flame and remove just before boiling. To make *dashi konbu*, kelp is dried in the sun, and then wrapped in straw mats. *Konbu* is rich in vitamins and minerals such as iodine. It also contains large quantities of potassium, which helps to reduce blood pressure. The best-known *konbu*-producing districts in Japan are Hidaka and Rausu in the northern island of Hokkaido. *Konbu* is not only used for *dashi*, but also for *tsukudani* and *tororo*.

Hijiki
Hijiki Seaweed

Hijiki is a porous, black seaweed with a surface that is less viscous but with more texture than other seaweeds. It is normally sold dried and should be reconstituted with water before use. *Hijiki* contains a lot of calcium, which can reduce nervousness and anxiety, and fibre, which is helpful for treating bowel disorders. It also contains a high level of iron, which is ideal for those who suffer from anaemia. As iron is absorbed by the body more easily when combined with Vitamin C, *hijiki* is best consumed with other vegetables.

Kanten

Agar Agar

Kanten is tasteless dried seaweed available in blocks, strands or powder form, which acts as a gelling agent. It is an ideal gelatin substitute for vegetarians. Delicious jellies can be made using fruit juice or milk and are popular in Japan as a healthy treat. High in fibre, kanten is good for treating constipation and reduces cholesterol levels as it helps prevent the bowel from absorbing cholesterol. Tokoroten, the natural gel form of kanten, is usually cut into thin strips and eaten cold with sweet or savoury dressings such as soy sauce and rice vinegar.

Kaiso

Other Seaweeds

A whole variety of seaweed products are used in Japan. Tororo konbu, used in soups, is made by soaking kelp in vinegar for a day to soften and then shaving it into flakes. Mozuku, a dark brown, viscous seaweed, is often eaten with rice vinegar as a starter, or palate refresher between courses. Aonori, small dried flakes of nori, are used as a garnish and commonly sprinkled on dishes such as yakisoba (fried noodles) and okonomiyaki (savoury pancakes). Mekabu, the base section of wakame, has a strong, salty flavour and contains a great amount of minerals.

Katsuobushi

Bonito Flakes

To make Katsuobushi, bonito fish fillets are salted and left to ferment and dry for four to six months before being shaved into fine flakes. For dashi, katsuobushi is usually added to konbu dashi. Konbu is heated in water on a medium heat then removed just before boiling. Katsuobushi is then added to the stock, which is brought to the boil then strained. Katsuobushi is also used as a topping for salads, tofu and cooked vegetables. There are varieties of katsuobushi which are especially made to be used as garnishes, Ito-kezuri is as thin as a piece of thread, and hana-katsuo is flat and as fine as a petal.

Iriko (Niboshi)

Dried Sardines for Stock

Iriko, dried katakuchi-iwashi (a small type of sardine), is also known as 'niboshi' which means 'boiled and dried', due to the way it is produced. It is used as a dashi ingredient for miso soup and Japanese stewed dishes. Unlike other dashi ingredients, iriko needs some preparation. To make iriko dashi, first the heads and internal organs of the iriko must be removed to avoid bitter and fishy smelling stock. Then, to bring out their taste, the iriko must be split in half, lengthwise, before being soaked in water. The pre-soaked iriko can then be put into water, brought to the boil and boiled for two to three minutes before straining.

Himono

Dried Seafoods

Himono literally means 'dried things', but is commonly refers to as dried seafood. They have more calcium, phosphorus, iron and potassium than raw seafood. Popular himono includes squid, sardine and horse-mackerel. Dried squid is so popular that it has a special name 'surume'. There are various ways of making himono; maruboshi describes fish that are dried after being soaked in salt water, while niboshi are dried after being boiled in salt water. Mirinboshi refers to seafood that is dried after being soaked in mirin.

Neri Seihin

Fish Cakes

Neri seihin, which literally means 'kneaded products', is a term used for pre-cooked fish cakes. Made from fish paste, neri seihin is an ideal food for those who do not have time to cook fish but still want to benefit from their nutrition. There are several kinds of neri seihin products with different ingredients and production methods. For example, to make kamaboko, fish paste is put on a small wooden board and steamed. For tsumire, sardine paste is boiled. Hanpen is boiled paste of white fish and other ingredients. Satsuma age is fried fish paste, sometimes with vegetables, and chikuwa is grilled fish paste.

VEGETABLES

Hakusai/Komatsuna/Shungiku
Green Vegetables

Many varieties of Japanese green vegetables are cultivated from winter to spring as they are vulnerable to the intense heat of summer. *Hakusai* (Chinese cabbage), *shungiku* (chrysanthemum leaves) and *komatsuna* (mustard spinach) all contain an abundance of carotene and Vitamin C. In particular, *komatsuna* has five times the calcium level of spinach. *Shungiku* is notable for its fragrant aroma. *Hakusai* and *komatsuna* are said to warm the body and protect against flu. These green vegetables are either cooked or boiled in soup. They lose volume when heated - which means that you can eat a lot and take in a multitude of vitamins in one meal!

Daikon/Gobo/Renkon
Root Vegetables

Japanese root vegetables are rich in vitamins and fibre. *Daikon* (Japanese radish) is white with a peppery taste. The leaf and stem contain more Vitamin C, calcium and iron than the root. It is eaten either grated (*daikon oroshi*) or as pickles (*takuan*). *Gobo* (burdock) is a thin, brown root with a distinct earthy flavour, which has a high fibre content that can help lower cholesterol. *Kinpira gobo* is a dish made from thin slices of *gobo*, cooked with carrots. *Renkon* lotus root has a reddish-brown skin and white flesh. The daily recommend amount of Vitamin C can be reached by eating 100 grams of this root vegetable.

Kyuri/Kabocha/Nasu
Cucumber/Pumpkin/Aubergine

Among popular varieties of *uri* (Japanese gourd) are *kyuri* (cucumber) and *kabocha* (pumpkin). *Kyuri* is smaller and thinner than cucumbers commonly used in the West and often used in salads and pickles. *Nippon-kabocha* (Japanese pumpkin) has a dark green skin and a sweet orange flesh, and is often simmered in soy sauce. *Seiyo-kabocha* (Western pumpkin) is sweeter and used in puddings, pies and potage. *Nasu* (Japanese aubergine) has a notable purple colour and is smaller than its Western equivalent. With its mild texture and slightly sweet taste, *nasu* is perfect for many different dishes such as *miso* soup, Chinese stir-fry, *tsukemono* and *yakinasu* (grilled *nasu*).

Yamaimo/Satoimo
Yam/Taro Root

Yamaimo (yam) and *satoimo* (taro root) have been cultivated in Japan since the Stone Age and provide high levels of Vitamin C and B1. Varieties of *yamaimo* include *nagaimo* (Chinese yam), *icho imo* (ginkgo yam, so called because the end of the plant spreads out like a ginkgo leaf) and round *yamato imo* (Japanese yam). *Yamaimo* is often grated into a pulpy consistency, mixed with flavouring and eaten with boiled rice. *Satoimo* is recognised by its brown fibre-like skin and greyish flesh. Its stickiness is said to help lower blood pressure and to reduce blood cholesterol levels.

Negi/Asatsuki/Nira
Vegetable Condiments

Negi (spring onion), *asatsuki* (a kind of chive) and *nira* (Chinese chive) have a strong, garlic-like aroma and flavour, and are often used to remove the odour of raw fish and meat. *Kizami-negi* (chopped spring onions) are sprinkled over *udon, soba* noodles and *miso* soup, and are used in *nabe* (hot-pot) for their body-heating quality. *Negi* and *asatsuki* can be used raw, as a fresh garnish for *hiyayakko* (chilled *tofu*). *Negi* is often cooked in combination with *yakitori* (grilled skewered chicken), and *nira* is used in the same way with liver.

Kinome/Shiso
Japanese Herbs

Japanese herbs are used as garnishes to add an aromatic finish to cooked food or soups. The use of herbs contrasts the Western style which uses several kinds of herbs in one dish. *Kinome* (young leaves of the *sansho* plant) adds a fresh, subtle minty flavour, used either fresh or dried. *Shiso* is a popular herb and is available in two types: *ao jisho* (green *shiso*), also called *oba,* which is used as a garnish for *sushi* and *sashimi* and can also be fried to make *tempura;* and purple-coloured *aka jiso* (red *shiso*), which is used in *umeboshi* or as dried flakes to add a savoury flavour to rice.

44

Kinoko

Mushrooms

Japan's most popular mushroom is the delicious *shiitake*. This flavoursome, slightly chewy mushroom, popular in both fresh and dried form, has anti-carcinogenic properties and contains vitamins B and D, which lowers blood pressure. *Matsutake*, a mushroom long prized as an autumn luxury food, has a wonderfully rich aroma and subtle taste. *Shimeji*, which comes in clusters and has a light texture, is also very popular. *Nameko* is small and amber-coloured, with a slippery surface. Popular dishes which use all of these mushrooms include *takikomi-gohan*, *kinoko-nabe* (mushroom hot-pot), *miso* soup and *osuimono*.

Sansai

Edible Wild Plants

Edible wild plants are widely loved in Japan as they mark the advent of spring. For example, *fuki*, which resembles asparagus and is high in fibre, and *udo*, which belongs to the ginseng family and whose soft stalks also look like asparagus. Two more examples are: *warabi*, the shoot of a certain kind of fern whose shiny triangle-shaped leaves are also edible, and *zenmai*, another edible fern named for its coiled leaves (*zenmai* literally means 'spiral spring'). The most popular of all these plants is *takenoko*, the ivory-coloured crisp and tender shoot of bamboo. These vegetables are cooked in a variety of ways and used in the making of many traditional Japanese dishes.

Kudamono/Kinomi

Japanese Fruits/Nuts

Kaki, the Japanese persimmon, is a round, orange-coloured sweet fruit which can be eaten raw and is very rich in vitamins. *Shibugaki* is another kind of persimmon which is very bitter fresh, but becomes sweet when its bitter tannin has been removed by drying. *Biwa* is another orange-coloured sweet fruit which is eaten raw. *Ginnan*, the bite-sized nuts of the ginkgo tree, are popular as an ingredient of *chawan-mushi* (savoury egg custard), and *kuri*, the Japanese chestnut, is especially popular roasted. *Kuri-kinton* (mashed sweet potato with sweetened *kuri*) is a popular *osechi-ryori* dish (special dishes for the New Year celebration).

Kanpyo

Gourd Shavings

Kanpyo is a unique traditional food made from gourds which have been shaved into ribbons then dried. With large amounts of iron, phosphorus and calcium, *kanpyo* is a nutritionally well-balanced food which can help prevent colon cancer by shortening the length of time carcinogens stay in the large intestine. It can also be effective in treating diabetes, arteriosclerosis, high blood pressure and constipation. *Kanpyo* should be washed, rubbed and softened with a spoonful of salt, then soaked in fresh water for a few minutes. It is then boiled for several minutes or simmered in stock to add flavour. It is used in various dishes including *maki-zushi* (rolled *sushi*).

Kiriboshi Daikon

Dried Slivered Radish

Daikon is a root vegetable which is very beneficial to the digestion which also contains a large amount of Vitamin C. *Kiriboshi daikon* is its dried form which can be bought or made at home. To make *kiriboshi daikon*, all you need to do is peel off the skin, cut it into long strips and dry it in the sun for a day or two. It can then be used throughout the year, after being reconstituted with water. It is used in various ways, for example in *tsukemono* or with soy sauce and *mirin* or sugar in *nimono* (simmered dishes).

Konnyaku/Shirataki

***Konnyaku* Jelly**

Konnyaku is a hard jelly made from the starch of the root or 'bulb' of the 'devil's tongue' plant and *shirataki* is its shredded form. With no distinctive taste, *konnyaku* and *shirataki* absorb the flavour and taste of the other ingredients they are cooked with. As both have next to no calories, they are ideal foods for those who want to watch their weight. They contain a type of dietary fibre which helps the body to discharge unnecessary and harmful substances. They can also be taken to help treat diabetes.

VEGETABLES/FRUITS
VEGETABLE FOODS

PRESERVED FOODS
NOODLES

Beni Shoga/Gari
Red/Pickled Ginger

The two most popular types of pickled ginger in Japan are *gari* and *beni shoga*. To prepare *gari*, thin slivers of the ginger root are used, and then pickled in plum vinegar which gives it a slightly sweet taste, pink colour and a pungent aroma. An essential condiment for *sushi*, it is said to refresh the palate between dishes. *Beni shoga* is similar to *gari*, but is red in colour and usually shredded. It is sprinkled on *okonomiyaki* (savoury pancakes), or *yakisoba* (stir-fried noodles). The medicinal effects are said to include improving indigestion, helping cure colds and cooling down high temperatures.

Umeboshi
Pickled Plum

Sun-dried, salted, then pickled with *shiso* (red perela leaves), *umeboshi* is a common everyday breakfast pickle in Japan, eaten with rice along with *miso* soup. Highly regarded in Japan both for its piquant taste and its medicinal properties, *umeboshi* is said to be extremely beneficial to the digestive system, and has been used for centuries to treat a broad range of ailments including food poisoning, flu, and hangovers. Delicious rice balls can be made by enclosing *umeboshi* in rice and wrapping it in *nori*, and can be used in a range of other dishes, in alcoholic drinks, and also makes a wonderful palate cleanser.

Tsukemono
Japanese Pickles

Nukazuke are made from fresh vegetables (such as cucumbers and Chinese cabbage), and are pickled in a pot of *nuka*. A stone is placed on top of the *nuka* container to weigh it down. Salt used in the pickling process helps the water in the vegetables to seep out, creating the characteristic texture of *tsukemono*. The pickles are usually eaten with rice as a side dish. There are many types of pickles including *sokuseki-zuke* (quickly prepared pickles), *kasu-zuke* (pickled in *sake* lees) and *koji-zuke* (pickled in malted rice).

Tsukudani
Preserved Seafood

Tsukudani is traditionally made from seaweed. Its name originates from Tsukudajima island, Tokyo, where it was first made in the Edo era but is now eaten all over Japan. Highly flavoured, *tsukudani* is usually eaten in small amounts with a bowl of boiled rice. The seaweed is cooked on a medium heat until most of the liquid is reduced, adding water at intervals to prevent scorching. Soy sauce is used in the cooking process along with *mirin* and *dashi* which preserve the ingredients naturally for 2 to 3 months. Nowadays, there are many variations, which are made from small fish and shellfish.

Udon
Wheat Noodles

Udon noodles are wonderfully thick and chewy. They are made from wheat flour kneaded with salt and water. Their texture can be adapted according to your taste by varying the cooking time, and are usually served in a hot broth, together with other ingredients such as prawn *tempura*, *abura age*, raw egg, and vegetables. They can also be served cold with a dipping sauce. They come in different widths and there is also a flattened variety called '*kishimen*' from the Nagoya region of Japan. It is available in dried, fresh, or pre-boiled form.

Soba
Buckwheat Noodles

Soba noodles are made from buckwheat flour. As buckwheat contains no gluten, wheat flour is usually added, although 100% buckwheat varieties are available. They come in fresh and dried forms, and can be eaten both hot and cold. *Soba* contain a type of carbohydrate that is easily digested and assimilated. *Soba* noodles also contain the rare Vitamin P, which helps to prevent high blood pressure, as well as the flavonoid 'rutin', which helps to thin the blood, thereby reducing the risk of heart disease. *Soba* noodles are extremely healthy and delicious .

Somen/Hiyamugi

Thin Wheat Noodles

Made from wheat flour kneaded with salt and water, *somen* noodles are the thinnest of the Japanese noodles - just under 1.3 millimeters thick (uncooked). *Somen* are thought to acquire a better texture when dried and allowed to mature for up to three years. When over 1.3 millimeters thick, *somen* are known as '*hiyamugi*'. *Somen* and *hiyamugi* are commonly eaten cold, especially in summer, together with a dipping sauce and garnishes such as grated ginger and spring onion. To cook them, boil in plenty of water for about three minutes, and then cool under running water.They are also eaten hot in a broth, in which case the dish is referred to as 'nyumen'.

Ramen

Chinese Noodles

Although originally from China, the Japanese have adapted the dish of *ramen* and made it their own. *Ramen* noodles are made from wheat flour kneaded together with egg, salt and a special type of carbonated water. The noodles come in different styles, the most common being long and cylindrical, but there are also curled and flattened varieties. *Ramen* noodles are served in soup, of which there are three basic flavours: soy sauce, salt and *miso*. Ingredients such as pork, fried vegetables and seaweed are often added. *Ramen* noodles are also served cold in a summer dish called *hiyashi chuka*.

Sokuseki Fukuro Men

Instant Noodles

Sokuseki fukuro men are noodles packed in individual single-portion bags with small sachets of soup powder and condiments. When added to boiling water they are ready to eat in just a few minutes. *Ramen* noodles are often pre-fried and are the most popular dried variety and come with different flavours, e.g. *miso*, pork, prawn and *shoyu*. There are fresh-noodle varieties which are also available in *udon* and *soba* noodle form. Popular as snacks, instant noodles are extremely handy for busy people, and when combined with other ingredients, they make a very satisfying main meal.

Sokuseki Kappu Men

Instant Cup/Bowl Noodles

Sokuseki kappu men are single portion cups or cartons of pre-fried, dried noodles with sachets of soup and condiments which are available in a range of different flavours. To prepare *kappu men*, you simply add boiling water and wait for three minutes. The most popular of these tasty instant snacks is made with *ramen,* but *udon* and *soba kappu men* are also available. Since you need only an electric kettle and a fork to enjoy them, they are just the thing for the workplace, busy times or 'emergencies'.

Sokuseki Misoshiru

Instant *Miso* Soup

Miso is an extremely nutritious paste made from soy beans, and has been used for hundreds of years in Japan. Today instant *misoshiru* (*miso* soup), prepared by simply adding boiling water, is used widely among those too busy to cook soup for only one person. A pack of instant *miso* soup usually contains *miso* paste or powder and separate dried ingredients such as *tofu*, *abura age*, *wakame* and vegetables. There are many kinds of instant *miso* soup made using different kinds of *miso* and various other ingredients.

Sokuseki Osuimono

Instant Broth

Osuimono is a Japanese soup with a delicate, subtler taste and more transparent appearance than the famous *miso* soup. Based on *dashi*, its mild flavour allows the taste and aroma of the added ingredients to be appreciated. Popular ingredients for *osuimono* include *matsutake* mushroom, sea bream, egg and *fu*. Since it is quite difficult to make it taste just right, instant *osuimono* is a very popular and convenient option. Simply put the dried ingredients into a bowl, pour on boiling water and mix. Disposable-cup type instant *osuimono* is also available.

Sokuseki Gohan/Sekihan
Instant Cooked White/Red Rice

In Japan, the most popular way to serve rice is simply to boil 'Japonica' rice until it is soft and slightly sticky, then put it into bowls, using a special scoop for a nice smooth round shape. On festive occasions, *sekihan*, rice cooked with red beans, is often served. Although in Japan the image of warm cooked rice is often associated with motherly love or happy families, ready-to-eat rice has nowadays become quite popular, especially among young people. The most popular form of ready-cooked rice can be stored at room temperature, and is pre-cooked and pre-packaged for microwave heating.

Sokuseki Okayu/Zosui
Instant Rice Porridge

Okayu and *zosui* are two different kinds of rice porridge. The basic *okayu* is a simple rice porridge seasoned with salt, but variations can be made using ingredients such as egg, salted salmon and *umeboshi*. As *okayu* is very easily digested, it is an ideal dish for those who have a weak stomach. Usually cooked with meat, vegetables and mushrooms, *zosui* is more like risotto than porridge. After eating *nabe*, a tasty and highly nutritious quick-cooking stew, rice is often put into the leftovers to make *zosui*. Most of the ready-to-eat *okayu* and *zosui* come in vacuum-packed sachets and can be boiled in the bag in just a few minutes.

Takikomi-gohan/Sushimeshi no Moto
Premix of *Takikomi-gohan*/*Sushi* Rice

Premixed *takikomi-gohan* (rice cooked with vegetables and mushrooms) is available in a dried or vacuum-packed form and there are many different kinds with varying ingredients. Premixed *sushi* rice products are very convenient and useful for those who want to make *sushi* at home. To make authentic *sushi* rice, all added ingredients have to be in just the right proportions, so using a premix is a far easier option. It is available in powdered form or as a vacuum-packed liquid. Premixes of *gomoku chirashi-zushi* (*sushi* rice mixed with vegetables) are also available.

Ochazuke no Moto
Premix of *Ochazuke*

Ochazuke, literally means 'rice in tea' is a popular light meal or snack frequently eaten after drinking alcohol or when one feels like eating something late in the evening. The dish consists of ingredients such as grilled salmon, *umeboshi* and *nori* on a bowl of rice, which you then pour green tea over. Alternatively, you can make *ochazuke* using a premixed *ochazuke* which contains powder and small dried pieces made up from ingredients such as *nori*, salmon, *goma*, *umeboshi*, *wasabi*, *sansai*, *arare*. There are many kinds of premixed *ochazuke* containing a variety of different ingredients.

Furikake
Toppings for Rice

Furikake is a savoury condiment which comes in powder or flake form in shakers, bags or in individual sachets. It is used as a topping to add both taste and nutritional value to boiled rice, as well as improving its appearance. There are many different varieties of *furikake*, made from such dried foods as fish, seaweed, *shiso*, *ume*, egg and sesame seeds. To make salmon *furikake*, for example, salmon is first cooked, then dried and ground into small flakes. Sesame seeds and *nori* flakes are then added.

Kare/Shichu no Ru
Roux of Curry/Stew

Introduced to the country by British traders in the 19th century, curry and rice is very popular in Japan. Today, it is usually made by frying and boiling the meat and vegetables then adding a premixed curry roux. There are many varieties of roux, with tastes ranging from mild to very hot and spicy - mixing two different kinds of roux is sometimes a good idea. Pre-cooked vacuum-packed curries with meat and vegetables are an even easier option. Similarly, there are pre-cooked and roux stews.

Tempurako

Tempura Flour

Composed of wheat flour, baking powder, egg powder and other ingredients, *tempura* flour is made into a batter, which can be used to make wonderfully crispy Japanese fritters, called *tempura*. Since it is quite difficult to make perfect *tempura*, it is better to use a premix. *Tempurako* will give *tempura* the unique crispy texture and keep the flavour of the ingredients it coats such as prawns, aubergine and shiitake mushrooms. Although *tempurako* is basically made for *tempura*, it can be also used for *okonomiyaki* (savoury pancake containing vegetables and meat or fish) to add a lighter texture.

Katakuriko

Dogtooth Violet Starch/Potato Starch

Katakuriko, taken from the dogtooth violet plant, is a white powder without any taste or smell and is used to thicken soups and sauces. Another way of using *katakuriko* is to mix it with spices and lightly sprinkle it over pieces of chicken or other ingredients before deep-frying them. *Katakuriko* is used in many ways and helps keep the nutrients and the taste of the ingredients in the food. Nowadays, potato starch or cornstarch are often used as a substitute for *katakuriko*, since natural dogtooth violet starch is now very expensive.

Joshinko

Rice Starch

Joshinko is a pure-white rice powder made from *uruchi-mai* (a kind of non-glutinous rice). The rice is washed with water and then milled with a roller. It is used for many kinds of Japanese sweets including *dango* (dumpling cake), *manju* (bun with bean paste filling) and *mochi-gashi* (rice cake sweets). *Joshinko* has a fine texture, and it can maintain the moisture of the ingredients. Although it is usually used exclusively for Japanese sweets, it can also be used as batter for fritters, or powder to thicken sauces. It is an excellent alternative for those who have an allergy to flour.

FLOUR/STARCH

Panko

Bread Crumbs

Panko are bread crumbs used with batter for deep-fried fritters. They are available both in dry and fresh forms. Fresh *panko* make the fritters lighter and softer than dried *panko*, as they contain more moisture which evaporates and forms small air holes when the *panko* are deep-fried. Dried *panko* can become similar to fresh *panko* when lightly moisturised by a water spray right before cooking. When cooking with dried *panko,* they must be applied evenly to the surface of your meat, fish, etc. To ensure freshness, dried *panko* should be stored in a cool and dry place.

Wantan/Gyoza/Shumai no Kawa

Wonton/Dumpling Skin

Originating in China, dumpling skins are used to make wonton (finger-size dumplings), *gyoza* (fried dumplings) and *shumai* (steamed dumplings), and are very popular in Japan. The skins used to wrap the fillings look quite similar to each other, but differ in size and ingredients. Wonton skins are square and yellowish in colour, and made from flour, egg, water, salt and an alkaline water called '*kansui*'. *Gyoza* skins are plain white, round in shape and made mainly from flour. *Shumai* skins are white, square, and the same size as wonton skins but they do not contain *kansui*.

Fu

Gluten Cake

Made from dried wheat gluten, *fu* is a highly digestible spongy dough and is available in various forms, including fresh (*nama-fu*) or roasted (*yaki-fu*). Originating in China, *fu* has been produced in Japan for hundreds of years. It is used in a number of Japanese dishes such as *miso* soup, *osuimono* and *sukiyaki* (dish of beef, vegetables and other ingredients cooked in a special pan). It has been recognised as a precious source of protein in '*kaiseki ryori*' or '*shojin ryori*' (traditional Buddhist-style vegetarian dishes).

Reito Sushi Neta

Frozen Toppings for *Sushi*

Sushi, one of the best known Japanese dishes, are small oblong balls of hand-rolled rice topped with various ingredients – usually slices of raw fish. *Sushi neta* is a common term used for *sushi* toppings. Popular *sushi neta* toppings can be categorised into the following: 'red meat' and 'white meat' fish, shellfish, roe and others. These include tuna, salmon, sole, sea bream, squid, octopus, prawn, scallop, bearded clam, salmon roe, sea urchin as well as many other types of seafood. Since many of *sushi neta* are uncooked seafood, they are very healthy and contain various nutrients, which help to reduce cholesterol - which is possibly why there is such a low rate of heart disease in Japan.

Reito Souzai

Frozen Ready Meals

Souzai is a term for Japanese everyday side dishes. Often put in lunchboxes, typical *souzai* include *tempura*, croquettes, cutlets, omelettes, spring rolls, fried fish, *gyoza* and *shumai*. Frozen *souzai*, which can be cooked in the microwave or oven, are a popular and convenient option for busy working parents who need to prepare lunchboxes for their children. Fried foods such as croquettes, spring rolls and *tempura* are particularly popular frozen *souzai*, as it takes a lot of time and effort to make these foods from scratch.

Senbei/Arare

Rice Crackers

Senbei and *arare* are traditional snacks that have been consumed in Japan for over 1,200 years. *Senbei* are crispy crackers made from Japonica rice. They are usually flat in shape, and are fried or (traditionally) baked over charcoal, which gives them their distinctive aroma. There are many varieties of *senbei*, such as salted, soy sauce flavoured, sesame coated, shrimp flavoured, with soy beans or nuts mixed in, sugar puffed and *norimaki* (wrapped in seaweed). *Arare* are smaller bite-sized versions of *senbei,* but are made from glutinous rice. They too come in a variety of flavours and colours.

Dagashi

Japanese Biscuits/Sweets

Dagashi, literally meaning 'cheap sweets', are assorted traditional confectionary. Originally, *dagashi* were produced by common people during the course of their everyday lives - their traditional unrefined shapes and old-time countryside flavours still appeal to Japanese people today. There are various kinds of *dagashi*, *karinto* are made from wheat and sugar, then fried and coated with melted brown sugar. *Boro*, biscuits made from wheat, buckwheat, or potato starch with egg, were brought to Japan from Portugal around 450 years ago. *Mamegashi*, which come in many varieties, are made from soy beans, peanuts and other beans or nuts coated with wheat or sugar, and are crispy and puffy in texture.

Wagashi

Japanese Traditional Cakes

Wagashi are traditional confectionery that are considered delicacies in Japan. The making of *wagashi* is a fine art, as their shape and design are as important as their taste. An integral part of the traditional Japanese tea ceremony, each *wagashi* often represents one of the seasons or a locality. They contain local and seasonal ingredients such as fruits and vegetables and are categorised according to cooking methods and ingredients. Some examples are rice cake, steamed, baked, and jelly *wagashi*. There are also half-dried and dried types, which keep for longer. Using only natural ingredients *wagashi* are far healthier than the average sweet.

Kashi Pan

Filled/Topped Breads

Kashi pan is the name given to Japanese filled/topped breads (*kashi* means sweet and *pan* means bread). There are several kinds of *kashi pan,* for example, *an-pan* is a sweet bread created over 130 years ago. An-pan's dough is fermented with a special Japanese rice-yeast and it has an *anko* filling. Another variety, *kare-pan* is deep fried and has a curry paste inside. *Melon-pan* is a sweet bread, shaped like and flavoured with melon, and has a sweet crunchy surface. *Mushi-pan* is a kind of steamed cake that comes in several different flavours such as cheese and green tea. *Kashi pan* is well loved by the Japanese and is very popular as a snack.

Japanese Food Products/Manufactures & Distributors

日本食品製造／取扱会社

CALIFORNIA
SUSHI RICE

錦

NEW VARIETY RICE
MEDIUM GRAIN

SPECIALLY SELECTED

NISHIKI
PREMIUM RICE

SETTING THE STANDARD
FOR PREMIUM RICE NISHIKI

総輸入販売元：

JFC (UK) LTD.

最高級新品種
カリフォルニア米
特撰錦米

Kome (Hakumai)
Japonica Rice

Ginmai-Ya Ltd.

PRODUCT(S): Kokuho Rose (USA), Maruyu (USA), Kaho (USA)
ADDRESS: Unit9-10, Southall Enterprise Centre, Bridge Rd. Southall UB2 4AB UK
TEL: +44-(0)20-8723-4551
FAX: +44-(0)20-8571-3600
E-MAIL: geoffrey3@tinyonline.co.uk
WEB: N/A
DISTRIBUTION: Contact company directly

Harro Foods Ltd.

PRODUCT(S): Sun Rice Koshihikari (Australia), Hikari (USA), Akitakomachi (USA)
ADDRESS: 23A Lombard Rd. Merton, London SW19 3TZ UK
TEL: +44-(0)20-8543-3343
FAX: +44-(0)20-8542-1962
E-MAIL: ikubo@harro.co.uk
WEB: http://www.harro.co.uk
DISTRIBUTION: Contact company directly

Honda Trading Europe Ltd.

PRODUCT(S): Akitakomachi (USA), Koshihikari (USA)
ADDRESS: Chiseldon House, Stone Hill Green, Westlea, Swindon SN5 7HB UK
TEL: +44-(0)1793-608-100
FAX: +44-(0)1793-527-802
E-MAIL: Shigeo-Seki@hntre.co.jp
WEB: N/A
DISTRIBUTION: Contact company directly

JFC (UK) Ltd.

PRODUCT(S): Nishiki premium medium grain rice (USA), Tamanishiki super premium short grain rice (USA)
ADDRESS: Unit 3, 1000 North Circular Rd. London NW2 7JP UK
TEL: +44-(0)20-8450-4626
FAX: +44-(0)20-8452-3734
E-MAIL: jfcuk@jfc.co.uk
WEB: http://www.jfc.com
DISTRIBUTION: Contact company directly

Nishiki is the premium quality of Californian medium grain rice, which is praised by food specialists around the world. Nishiki is a new variety of rice which surpasses the aroma, flavour and texture of any other of its class. Nishiki's favourable sensory characteristics are achieved by maturing every grain to its peak, and gently milling and packaging it to prevent breakage. This is why Nishiki exceeds far beyond the top grade set by the USDA standards. Nishiki rice is guaranteed to satisfy the most uncompromising of customers, because they are setting the standards for premium medium grain rice - NISHIKI.

Kaigai Tsusho Ltd.

PRODUCT(S): Minori (Spain)
ADDRESS: 44 Coombe Rd. Kingston, Surrey KT2 7AF UK
TEL: +44-(0)20-8549-8076
FAX: +44-(0)20-8547-1216
E-MAIL: N/A
WEB: N/A
DISTRIBUTION: Contact company directly

Sumitomo Corporation Europe plc

PRODUCT(S): SunRice Koshihikari (Australia)
ADDRESS: Vintners' Pl. 68 Upper Thames St. London EC4V 3BJ UK
TEL: +44-(0)20-7246-3785
FAX: +44-(0)20-7246-3936
E-MAIL: glenn.clark@sumitomocorp.co.uk
WEB: http://www.sumitomocorp.co.uk
DISTRIBUTION: Harro Foods ☞See p.74

SunRice Koshihikari is a short grain white rice with a soft sticky texture and glossy appearance when cooked. Ideal for Sushi, Nori rolls and Rice balls although it goes well with other Asian dishes. It is one of the most recent varieties to be grown in Australia. The Koshihikari was developed from a prized Japanese variety originally imported from Japan in the 1960's. The rice is grown in a sunny unpolluted environment, and rotation farming practices have kept it free of diseases. Australian rice growers use the most technologically advanced farming practices, harvesting and storage techniques which result in them being able to supply the highest quality rice available.

Tazaki Foods Ltd.

PRODUCT(S): Yutaka (USA), Akitakomachi (USA), Koshihikari (Japan)
ADDRESS: 2 Dundee Way, Mollison Ave. Enfield, Middlesex EN3 7NJ UK
TEL: +44-(0)20-8344-3001
FAX: +44-(0)20-8344-3003
E-MAIL: info@tazakifoods.com
WEB: http://www.tazakifoods.com
DISTRIBUTION: Contact company directly

Tomen Foods UK Ltd.

PRODUCT(S): Koshihikari mai "Daichi" (USA)
ADDRESS: 27-29 Brunel Rd. London W3 7XR UK
TEL: +44-(0)20-8749-1515
FAX: +44-(0)20-8749-0550
E-MAIL: kurahara@ldn.tomen.co.uk
WEB: http://www.tomenfoods.co.uk
DISTRIBUTION: Contact company directly

Yoshikawa UK Ltd.

PRODUCT(S): Kitanoshinju (China)
ADDRESS: Unit 6-7, The Chase Centre, 8 Chase Rd. London NW10 6QD UK
TEL: +44-(0)20-8453-1001
FAX: +44-(0)20-8453-0606
E-MAIL: tktrade@japan-foods.co.uk
WEB: http://www.japan-foods.co.uk
DISTRIBUTION: Contact company directly

Genmai
Japonica Brown Rice

Domer, Inc.

PRODUCT(S): Pre-germinated whole rice
ADDRESS: 3-3-19 Tokiwagi, Ueda-shi, Nagano 386-0027 Japan
TEL: +81-(0)268-28-6611
TEL: +81-(0)268-28-6616
E-MAIL: tsukahara@muf.biglobe.ne.jp
WEB: http://www.hatsuga.com
DISTRIBUTION: Contact company directly

Domer Inc. has been researching and producing pre-germinated whole rice and related products in partnership with the Japanese Ministry of Agriculture since 1995. Pre-germination, which causes the rice to sprout, greatly increases its nutritional value making it far richer in antioxidants and essential vitamins and minerals than white rice and even conventional brown rice. The company, which produces over 200 tons of the rice a month from its plant in Nagano prefecture, Japan, produces a range of related products in addition to the pre-germinated rice in its basic form. These include cereals, crackers, breads and supplements.

Sake
Rice Wine

Akashi Hakko Kogyo Inc.

PRODUCT(S): Funage no onikoroshi
DISTRIBUTION: Harro Foods ☞See p.74

Akita Seishu Inc.

PRODUCT(S): Dewatsuru
DISTRIBUTION: Tazaki Foods ☞See p.74

Asabiraki Co., Ltd.

PRODUCT(S): Yumeakari, Nanburyu
DISTRIBUTION: JFC UK ☞See p.74

TASTE THE TREASURE OF JAPAN

Japan Prestige Sake Association
Committed to bringing the finest sake to the world

男山 OTOKOYAMA
白瀧 SHIRATAKI
司牡丹 TSUKASABOTAN

飛良泉 HIRAIZUMI
天寿玉 KUSUDAMA
美少年 BISHONEN

一人娘 HITORI MUSUME
月の桂 TSUKINO KATSURA
大山 OHYAMA

悠の譽 KOSHINO HOMARE
菊姫 KIKUHIME
澤乃井 SAWANOI

明眸 MEIBO
梅錦 UMENISHIKI
真澄 MASUMI

酒呑童子 SHUTENDOJI
刈穂 KARIHO
若鶴鬼ころし WAKATAKE ONIKOROSHI

酔心 SUISHIN
浦霞 URAKASUMI
若戎 WAKA-EBIS

鳴門鯛 NARUTOTAI
腰古井 KOSHIGOI
賀茂泉 KAMOIZUMI

新政 ARAMASA
峰乃白梅 MINENO HAKUBAI
五橋 GOKYO

一ノ蔵 ICHINOKURA
萬歳樂 MANZAIRAKU
天盃 TENPAI

開華 KAIKA
春鹿 HARUSHIKA
西の關 NISHINOSEKI

日本名門酒会
JAPAN PRESTIGE SAKE ASSOCIATION

Aramasa Shuzo Co., Ltd.

PRODUCT(S): Aramasa (Towazugatari sake, Suisen junmai sake, Ginko sake)
ADDRESS: 6-2-35 Omachi, Akita-shi, Akita 010-0921 Japan
TEL: +81-(0)18-823-6407
FAX: +81-(0)18-864-4407
E-MAIL: N/A **WEB:** N/A
DISTRIBUTION: Okanaga Europe, Harro Foods, Tazaki Foods ☞See p.74

Towazugatari sake is an elegant sake - mild, with a clear aroma. It is a fine, pure sake, containing no added alcohol or sugar. This purity comes from the famous Akita prefecture Miyama-Nishiki brand of rice which is used in this special sake. Suisen Junmai sake, also containing no additives, is full of the delicious flavour of both Miyama-Nishiki and Kiyo-Nishiki superior rice. It has a delicate scent with a full flavour that is very satisfying to drink. Ginko sake has an abundant, clear and lively aroma. It is light and beautiful and its flavour swells with refinement.

Asahi Sake Brewery Co., Ltd.

PRODUCT(S): Kubota (Senju, Manju)
DISTRIBUTION: Tazaki Foods ☞See p.74

Bishonen Sake Co., Ltd.

PRODUCT(S): Bishonen
DISTRIBUTION: Okanaga Europe, Harro Foods, Tazaki Foods ☞See p.74

Chiyomusubi Sake Brewery Co., Ltd.

PRODUCT(S): Rikasuimei, Oni no shitaburui
DISTRIBUTION: JFC UK ☞See p.74

Daiichi Shuzo Co., Ltd.

PRODUCT(S): Kaika
DISTRIBUTION: Okanaga Europe, Harro Foods ☞See p.74

Daimon Sake Brewing Co., Ltd.

PRODUCT(S): Rikyubai
DISTRIBUTION: Tazaki Foods ☞See p.74

Daishichi Sake Brewery Co., Ltd.

PRODUCT(S): Daishichi
DISTRIBUTION: Okanaga Europe, Harro Foods, JFC UK ☞See p.74

Godo Shusei Co., Ltd.

PRODUCT(S): Hana no tomo

DISTRIBUTION: Harro Foods ☞See p.74

Hakkai Sake Celler Corporation

PRODUCT(S): Hakkaisan
DISTRIBUTION: JFC UK ☞See p.74

Hakutsuru Sake Brewing Co., Ltd.

PRODUCT(S): Hakutsuru (Junmai dai ginjo, Junmai ginjo, Draft sake, Plum wine)
ADDRESS: 4-5-5 Sumiyoshiminami-machi, Higashinada-ku, Kobe-shi 658-0041 Japan
TEL: +81-(0)78-822-8903
FAX: +81-(0)78-841-8332
E-MAIL: exports@hakutsuru.co.jp
WEB: http://www.hakutsuru-sake.com
DISTRIBUTION: Contact company directly

Established in 1743, Hakutsuru Sake Brewing Company Ltd. has grown to become one of the largest brewers of Sake in Japan, with an annual turnover of 42,300 million yen. It has reached its present position largely through combining the traditional Sake making techniques of its past with the latest developments in brewing technology. The company now offers a range of Sakes, including premium quality Sakes that have earned a good reputation among their long-established customers, as well as boxed Sake, mirin (sweet cooking Sake), shochu (Japanese spirit), and imported wines.

Hiraizumi Honpo Co., Ltd.

PRODUCT(S): Hiraizumi
DISTRIBUTION: Okanaga Europe, Harro Foods ☞See p.74

Hokusetsu Sake Brewery Co., Ltd.

PRODUCT(S): Nobu (Daiginjo, Junmai daiginjo)
ADDRESS: 2377-2 Tokuwa, Akadomari-mura, Sado-gun, Niigata 952-0706 Japan
TEL: +81-(0)259-87-3500
FAX: +81-(0)259-87-3173
E-MAIL: hokusetu@sado.co.jp
WEB: http://www.sado.co.jp/hokusetu
DISTRIBUTION: Nobu ☞See p.81

Hokusetsu Sake Brewry Co., Ltd. has been brewing sake on the small Japanese island of Sado since

---

1886. The company produces uncompromisingly dry sakes, many of which have been awarded Japan's most coveted prizes for brewing. Having gained fame in Japan, Hokusetsu began exporting its products to the United States in 1990 and soon became established as the sake brewer for Nobu Matsushisa's renowned chain of restaurants. Whilst most sakes in Japan are now industrially produced, Hokusetsu's sakes are still made almost entirely by hand, and the success of the brewing process is left entirely to the experience of the company's master brewer.

Ichinokura Sake Brew. Co., Ltd.

PRODUCT(S): Ichinokura
DISTRIBUTION: Okanaga Europe, Tazaki Foods ☞See p.74

Ippongi Kubohonten Co., Ltd.

PRODUCT(S): Denshin, Ippongi
DISTRIBUTION: JFC UK ☞See p.74

Ishibashi Shuzo Co.

PRODUCT(S): Itten, Yashiorino sake
DISTRIBUTION: JFC UK ☞See p.74

Kaetsu Sake Brewing Co., Ltd.

PRODUCT(S): Kirin
DISTRIBUTION: Tazaki Foods ☞See p.74

Kamoizumi Shuzo Co., Ltd.

PRODUCT(S): Kamoizumi
DISTRIBUTION: Okanaga Europe, Harro Foods ☞See p.74

Kamotsuru Sake Brewing Co., Ltd.

PRODUCT(S): Kamotsuru
DISTRIBUTION: Tazaki Foods ☞See p.74

Katoh Kahachiroh Shuzo Co., Ltd.

PRODUCT(S): Ohyama
DISTRIBUTION: Okanaga Europe, Tazaki Foods ☞See p.74

Kayashima Shuzo Co., Ltd.

PRODUCT(S): Nishinoseki
DISTRIBUTION: Okanaga Europe, Harro Foods ☞See p.74

Kenbishi Sake Brewery Co., Ltd.

PRODUCT(S): Kenbishi
DISTRIBUTION: Tazaki Foods ☞See p.74

Kikusui Co., Ltd.

PRODUCT(S): Kikusui
DISTRIBUTION: JFC UK ☞See p.74

King Jozo

PRODUCT(S): Banshu nishiki
DISTRIBUTION: Harro Foods ☞See p.74

Kiku-Masamune Sake Brewing Co., Ltd.

PRODUCT(S): Kiku-Masamune (Sake junmai, Taru sake, Sake deluxe, Junmai ginjyo)
ADDRESS: 1-7-15 Mikage-Honmachi, Higashinada-ku, Kobe-shi 658-0046 Japan
TEL: +81-(0)78-854-1042
FAX: +81-(0)78-854-1001
E-MAIL: y-nagao@kikumasamune.co.jp
WEB: http://www.kikumasamune.com
DISTRIBUTION: Contact company directly

Kiku-Masamune Sake Brewing Co., Ltd. has been brewing sake for 340 years since its foundation in Kobe in 1659. The range of Kiku-Masamune Sakes are highly regarded for the quality of their ingredients and clean, full-bodied flavour. Particularly renowned for its dry sakes and famous for a commitment to quality, the company now exports its sake worldwide. The current range includes a premium quality sake and Taru Sake, a sake aged in Cedar wood casks for a distinctive flavour. Kiku-Masamune hopes to introduce a broader appreciation of finest quality Japanese sake in the UK.

Kobori Shuzoten Co., Ltd.

PRODUCT(S): Manzairaku
DISTRIBUTION: Okanaga Europe ☞See p.74

Koikawa Shuzo Co., Ltd.

PRODUCT(S): Koikawa
DISTRIBUTION: JFC UK ☞See p.74

Masuda Sake Brewing Co., Ltd.

PRODUCT(S): Masuizumi
DISTRIBUTION: Tazaki Foods ☞See p.74

Miyasaka Brewing Co., Ltd.

PRODUCT(S): Masumi
ADDRESS: 1-16 Motomachi, Suwa-shi, Nagano 392-8686 Japan
TEL: +81-(0)266-52-6161
FAX: +81-(0)266-53-4477
E-MAIL: naotaka-miyasaka@masumi.co.jp
WEB: http://www.masumi.co.jp
DISTRIBUTION: Okanaga Europe, Tazaki Foods ☞See p.74

Miyazaki Honten Brewery Co., Ltd.

PRODUCT(S): Miyanoyuki
DISTRIBUTION: JFC UK ☞See p.74

Miyozakura Jouzou, Inc.

PRODUCT(S): Miyozakura

DISTRIBUTION: Tazaki Foods ☞See p.74

Morita Co., Ltd.

PRODUCT(S): Nenohi koyoi pack, Onikoroshi
DISTRIBUTION: Harro Foods ☞See p.74

Nanbu Bijin Co., Ltd.

PRODUCT(S): Nanbu Bijin tokubetsu junmaishu
ADDRESS: 13 Kamimachi, Fukuoka, Ninohe-shi, Iwate 028-6101 Japan
TEL: +81-(0)195-23-3133
FAX: +81-(0)195-23-4713
E-MAIL: sake@nanbubijin.co.jp
WEB: http://www.nanbubijin.co.jp
DISTRIBUTION: Tazaki Foods ☞See p.74

Nanbu Bijin sake is a name recognised throughout Japan and the world, as a superior beverage that has won many accolades. In the international sake contest, "Mond Selection", Nanbu Bijin has continued to receive the Grand Gold Medal since 1997. The majority of rice used in making Nanbu Bijin is cultivated in the Iwate Prefecture area, which is renowned for its quality in the production of sake. The purest of water is used in the hand made brewing process to result in a superior balance between soft, delicate tones and a sharp, full-bodied sake.

Naniwa Shuzo

PRODUCT(S): Naniwa masamune
DISTRIBUTION: Harro Foods ☞See p.74

Nariwa Ozeki Shuzo Co., Ltd.

PRODUCT(S): Ohtouka, Ohkagura
DISTRIBUTION: JFC UK ☞See p.74

Ohmuraya Brewery Co., Ltd.

PRODUCT(S): Wakatake onikoroshi
DISTRIBUTION: Okanaga Europe, Tazaki Foods ☞See p.74

Otokoyama Co., Ltd.

PRODUCT(S): Otokoyama (Junmai daiginjo, Junmai utamaronatori, Junmai kuniyoshinatori)
ADDRESS: 2-7 Nagayama, Asahikawa-shi, Hokkaido 079-8412 Japan
TEL: +81-(0)166-48-3777
FAX: +81-(0)166-48-1940
E-MAIL: info@otokoyama.com
WEB: http://www.otokoyama.com
DISTRIBUTION: Okanaga Europe, Harro Foods, Tazaki Foods ☞See p.74

Otokoyama, first brewed in Itami during the 17th century, was favoured by the Tokugawa Shogun family as one of the finest sakes of the Edo period, and Utamaro, the renowned Ukiyoe (woodblock print) master, loved it so much that he depicted it in his works. Otokoyama's brewery is blessed with natural underground water originating from the perpetual snows of nearby Mt. Daisetu and an extremely cold climate paramount for brewing superb sake. Winning more medals than any other sake in Japan since 1877, Otokoyama has won successive awards in wine and spirit competitions around the world.

Ozawa Shuzo Co., Ltd.

PRODUCT(S): Sawanoi
DISTRIBUTION: Okanaga Europe, Harro Foods ☞See p.74

Ozeki Corporation

PRODUCT(S): Ozeki yamada nishiki
DISTRIBUTION: Tazaki Foods ☞See p.74

Ozeki Sake (U.S.A.), Inc.

PRODUCT(S): Ozeki (Sake, Hako no sake, Sake dry, Ginjo)
ADDRESS: 249 Hillcrest Rd. Hollister, CA 95023 USA
TEL: +1-831-637-9217
FAX: +1-831-637-0953
E-MAIL: yoshikae@ozekisake.com
WEB: http://www.ozekisake.com
DISTRIBUTION: JFC UK ☞See p.74

Combining a tradition since 1711 with modern technology, Ozeki sake became the first Japanese sake company to debut in America, in 1979. Made from special short grain American rice and the purest Sierra Nevada water, it is produced with superior brewing technology in Ozeki's very own rice mill. Three different types of sake ensure that there is an Ozeki sake to suit every connoisseur. Ginjo sake uses half refined rice, and is developed over forty days to create a fruity aroma. Ozeki Dry has a light but dry quality, whilst Ozeki Regular is full-bodied and smooth.

Rihaku Sake Brewing Co., Ltd.

PRODUCT(S): Rihaku
DISTRIBUTION: Tazaki Foods ☞See p.74

S. Imanishi Co., Ltd.

PRODUCT(S): Harushika
DISTRIBUTION: Okanaga Europe, Harro Foods, Tazaki Foods ☞See p.74

Sakai Shuzo Co., Ltd.

PRODUCT(S): Gokyo
DISTRIBUTION: Okanaga Europe, Tazaki Foods ☞See p.74

Sasaichi Shuzo Co., Ltd.

PRODUCT(S): Madoka
DISTRIBUTION: JFC UK ☞See p.74

Saura Co., Ltd.

PRODUCT(S): Honjikomi urakasumi, Junmai urakasumi, Junmai ginjo urakasumi zen
ADDRESS: 2-19 Motomachi, Shiogama-shi, Miyagi 985-0052 Japan
TEL: +81-(0)22-362-4165
FAX: +81-(0)22-362-7895
E-MAIL: info@urakasumi.com
WEB: http://www.urakasumi.com
DISTRIBUTION: Okanaga Europe, Harro Foods ☞See p.74

Urakasumi Zen sake is brewed from up to fifty percent refined and polished locally grown rice and our own special yeast, at a low temperature. Its mild and aromatic balance creates a distinctive fine rice wine. Cool it to your liking and enjoy it with a meal. Junmai Urakasumi sake's pure taste and natural rice flavour is achieved by brewing up to sixty-five percent local refined and polished rice, with no added alcohol or sugar. Saura Co., Ltd. also offers you Honjikomi Urakasumi sake, a softer sake with a characteristic clear aftertaste. You can enjoy the beautiful flavours of superior sake with any of Saura's varieties.

Seiryo Shuzo Co., Ltd.

PRODUCT(S): Iyo densetsu, Kijoshu seiryo
DISTRIBUTION: JFC UK ☞See p.74

Sekiya Jouzou Co., Ltd.

PRODUCT(S): Meibo
DISTRIBUTION: Okanaga Europe, Tazaki Foods ☞See p.74

Senkin Shuzo Co., Ltd.

PRODUCT(S): Nikko kirifuri, Ginyu sizuku, Kaishu
DISTRIBUTION: JFC UK ☞See p.74

Shirataki Sake Brewery Co., Ltd.

PRODUCT(S): Ginjo jozen mizu no gotoshi, Junmai uonuma, Junmai daiginjo
ADDRESS: 2640 Yuzawa, Yuzawa-machi, Minamiuonuma-gun, Niigata 949-6101 Japan
TEL: +81-(0)25-784-3443
FAX: +81-(0)25-785-5485
E-MAIL: kazu-maruyama@jozen.co.jp
WEB: http://www.jozen.co.jp
DISTRIBUTION: Okanaga Europe, Harro Foods, Tazaki Foods ☞See p.74

Ginjo Jozenmizunogotoshi sake has a fresh essence and a light sweet flavour, with a hint of tang. For first time drinkers, this elegant Japanese sake is smooth and easily appreciated. Junmai Uonuma sake is known for its mildness and smoothness and is free from added alcohol or sugar. Unique from other pure sakes, it is simple and easy to drink. It suits many different styles of cooking, and is an enjoyable, versatile beverage. Junmai Daiginjo Sake Shirataki also contains no additives and has a fruity taste and scent, like a touch of silk. Try this unique and new sake for yourself.

Sudo-Honke, Inc.

PRODUCT(S): Satono homare
DISTRIBUTION: Tazaki Foods ☞See p.74

Suehiro Sake Brewery Co., Ltd.

PRODUCT(S): Ken, Kira
DISTRIBUTION: JFC UK ☞See p.74

Suishin Yamane Honten & Co., Ltd.

PRODUCT(S): Suishin
DISTRIBUTION: Okanaga Europe, Tazaki Foods ☞See p.74

Syata-Syuzou Co., Ltd.

PRODUCT(S): Tengumai
DISTRIBUTION: Harro Foods, Tazaki Foods ☞See p.74

Takara Sake USA Inc.

PRODUCT(S): Shochikubai
DISTRIBUTION: Tazaki Foods ☞See p.74

Takasago Sake Brewing Co., Ltd.

PRODUCT(S): Kokushi musou
DISTRIBUTION: JFC UK ☞See p.74

Takeshita Honten Co., Ltd.

PRODUCT(S): Izumohomare
DISTRIBUTION: JFC UK ☞See p.74

Tamanohikari Sake Brewing Co., Ltd.

PRODUCT(S): Tamanohikari
DISTRIBUTION: JFC UK ☞See p.74

Tatsuuma-Honke Brewing Co., Ltd.

PRODUCT(S): Hakushika
DISTRIBUTION: Harro Foods ☞See p.74

Tentaka Sake Brewing Co., Ltd.

PRODUCT(S): Tentaka
DISTRIBUTION: Tazaki Foods ☞See p.74

Tenzan Sake Brewing Co., Ltd.

PRODUCT(S): Tenzan
DISTRIBUTION: Tazaki Foods ☞See p.74

Tosatsuru Sake Brewery Co., Ltd.

PRODUCT(S): Tosatsuru
DISTRIBUTION: Tazaki Foods ☞See p.74

Tsukasabotan Sake Brewing Co., Ltd.

PRODUCT(S): Tsukasabotan
DISTRIBUTION: Okanaga Europe, Harro Foods, Tazaki Foods ☞See p.74

Wakaebisu Shuzo Co., Ltd.

PRODUCT(S): Wakaebisu
DISTRIBUTION: Okanaga Europe ☞See p.74

Yaegaki Sake & Spirits, Inc.

PRODUCT(S): Yaegaki
DISTRIBUTION: Okanaga Europe, Harro Foods ☞See p.74

Yamagata Honten Co., Ltd.

PRODUCT(S): Moriko, Shoin, Kaori
DISTRIBUTION: JFC UK ☞See p.74

Yamamoto Honke Co., Ltd.

PRODUCT(S): Kaguyahime, Mizunoshirabe, Matsunomidori
DISTRIBUTION: JFC UK ☞See p.74

Yamanaka Shuzo Co., Ltd.

PRODUCT(S): Hitorimusume
DISTRIBUTION: Okanaga Europe, Harro Foods ☞See p.74

Yatsushika Brewery Co., Ltd.

PRODUCT(S): Yatsushika
DISTRIBUTION: JFC UK ☞See p.74

Yoshida Sake Brewing Co., Ltd.

PRODUCT(S): Izumo gassan
DISTRIBUTION: Tazaki Foods ☞See p.74

Yoshinogawa Sake Brewery Co., Ltd.

PRODUCT(S): Yoshinogawa
DISTRIBUTION: Tazaki Foods ☞See p.74

Biru
Japanese Beer

Asahi Beer Europe Ltd.

PRODUCT(S): Asahi beer super dry, Nikka whisky, Shochu Ichiban-fuda
ADDRESS: 17 Connaught Pl. London W2 2EL UK
TEL: +44-(0)20-7706-8330
FAX: +44-(0)20-7706-4220
E-MAIL: europe@asahibeer.co.uk
WEB: http://www.asahibeer.co.uk
DISTRIBUTION: Coors Brewers, Tazaki Foods
☞See p.74

Asahi has been brewing beer in Japan since 1889. Renowned for its pursuit of excellence and pioneering spirit, it introduced the first bottled draft beer to Japan at the start of the 20th century and the first canned beer in 1958. With its most famous product, the clean tasting 'Super Dry' beer, now successfully established as one of Japan's best selling beers, Asahi's reputation for quality, flavour and style has lead to an increasing popularity in the overseas market. Super Dry is now brewed in five countries and marketed and distributed in over forty countries world-wide.

Kirin Europe GmbH

PRODUCT(S): Japanese premium lager beer
ADDRESS: Louise-Dumont-Str. 31, 40211 Düsseldorf, Germany
TEL: +49-(0)211-353086
FAX: +49-(0)211-363996
E-MAIL: jun.arakawa@kirin.de
WEB: http://www.kirineurope.com
DISTRIBUTION: Charles Wells, JFC UK
☞See p.74

Kirin Beer has a pedigree dating back to 1888, when it was first brewed under the critical eye of the Japanese Master Brewers. Defined by its premium taste and elegant presentation, Kirin Beer derives its name from the mythical creature said to be part deer, part dragon and hailed to be the harbringer of good fortune. This classic lager is now on draught, and is the only draught Japanese beer available in the U.K. Kirin Beer is a Japanese lager, light in colour, with a distinc-

tive taste, smooth body and refreshingly subtle flavour. "A lager of great distinction." - Roger Protz, Editor of The Good Beer Guide.

Sapporo Breweries, Ltd.

PRODUCT(S): Sapporo premium lager, Draft beer
ADDRESS: 4-20-1 Ebisu, Shibuya-ku, Tokyo 150-8686 Japan
TEL: +81-(0)3-5423-7224
FAX: +81-(0)3-5423-2056
E-MAIL: Hiroshi.Sakai@sapporobeer.co.jp
WEB: http://www.sapporobeer.co.jp
DISTRIBUTION: Marblehead, Harro Foods, JFC UK, Tazaki Foods ☞See p.74

Since its establishment in 1876, Sapporo Breweries, Japan's oldest brewery, has continued to pursue its single aim - the production of the finest quality beer. Over a century later, consumers still appreciate the quality of Sapporo beer. The instantly recognisable 'Silver Can' is produced in Japan with Sapporo's own ceramic filtration technology and the Premium Lager is manufactured according to their specifications by the Diageo group in Ireland. Sapporo is known for using only the finest raw materials from the world's best known sources. This, together with their attention to detail, ensures that Sapporo beer always tastes smooth and rich with plenty of flavour.

Uisuki
Whisky

Nikka Whisky Distilling Co., Ltd.

PRODUCT(S): Nikka whisky
ADDRESS: 17 Connaught Pl. London W2 2EL UK
TEL: +44-(0)20-7706-9977
FAX: +44-(0)20-7706-9988
E-MAIL: london@nikka.com
WEB: http://www.nikka.com
DISTRIBUTION: Tazaki Foods ☞See p.74

Suntory Ltd.

PRODUCT(S): Suntory (Hibiki, Yamazaki 12years, Royal)
ADDRESS: 25 St James's St. London SW1A 1HA UK
TEL: +44-(0)20-7839-9370
FAX: +44-(0)20-7839-9379
E-MAIL: nobu@jais.co.jp
WEB: http://www.suntory.co.jp
DISTRIBUTION: JFC UK ☞See p.74

Shochu
Japanese Clear Spirit

Kagura Shuzo Ltd.

PRODUCT(S): Mugijochu himukano kurouma (Long term storage barley shochu)
DISTRIBUTION: Harro Foods ☞See p.74

Komasa Jyozo

PRODUCT(S): Windows shochu
ADDRESS: UK Agent: The Distinctive Drinks Company Ltd., The Old Dairy, Broadfield Rd. Sheffield S8 0XQ UK
TEL: +44-(0)114-255-2002
FAX: +44-(0)114-255-2005
E-MAIL: sales@distinctivedrinks.com
WEB: http://www.distinctivedrinks.com
DISTRIBUTION: Contact company directly

Kyushu is the most famous area in Japan for the production of shochu, especially sweet potato shochu. Its distinctive taste and aroma reflect over 500 years of tradition. Windows Shochu from the Distinctive Drinks Co. is packaged in an eye-catching bottle with an innovative window effect, through which a stunning painting by renowned Japanese artist Ichirou Tsuruta can be seen. Windows Shochu is made using the finest barley and sweet potato and then distilled leaving a fresh and smooth spirit that can be drunk straight or used in cocktails.

Sanwa Shurui Co., Ltd.

PRODUCT(S): Iichiko
DISTRIBUTION: Harro Foods, JFC UK, Tazaki Foods ☞See p.74

Satsuma Shuzo Co., Ltd.

PRODUCT(S): Satsuma shiranami, Kannoko
DISTRIBUTION: Harro Foods, Tazaki Foods ☞See p.74

Unkai Distillery Co., Ltd.

PRODUCT(S): Soba shochu (Unkai, Kuromaru), Mugi shochu kuromaru, Taiga no itteki, Nayuta no toki
DISTRIBUTION: Harro Foods, JFC UK, Tazaki Foods ☞See p.74

Umeshu
Plum Wine

Choya Umeshu GmbH (Deutschland)

PRODUCT(S): Choya umeshu (Dento, Dento herb), Choya plum
ADDRESS: Hanns-Martin-Schleyer-Str.43 D-47877 Willich, Germany
TEL: +49-(0)2154-48-98-10

FAX: +49-(0)2154-48-98-111
E-MAIL: info@choya.co.jp
WEB: http://www.choya.com
DISTRIBUTION: Contact company directly

Kikkoman Corporation

PRODUCT(S): Plum wine
DISTRIBUTION: JFC UK ☞See p.74

Ocha
Green Tea

Clearspring Ltd.

PRODUCT(S): Organic Japanese tea (Sencha, Kukicha, Bancha, Genmaicha)
DISTRIBUTION: Contact company directly ☞See p.71

Daigo Shoten & Co

PRODUCT(S): Marutomo (Sencha, Houjicha, Bancha, Genmaicha, Konacha)
DISTRIBUTION: Harro Foods ☞See p.74

Kisaku-en Co., Ltd.

PRODUCT(S): Sushicha konacha, Sencha gold, Sencha gold with macha, Genmaicha macha-iri, Konacha
DISTRIBUTION: JFC UK ☞See p.74

Maedaen

PRODUCT(S): Sencha, Kokyusencha, Josencha, Yamegyokuro, Genmaicha, Hojicha, Kukicha, Sweet greentea, Sencha green tea bag, Premium tea bag (Sencha, Genmaicha, Hojicha, Oolongcha), Mugicha reisui tea bag
DISTRIBUTION: JFC UK ☞See p.74

Shimodozono International GmbH

PRODUCT(S): KEIKO (Kabuse No.1, No.2, No.3, Tenko, Soshun, Tenbu, Tenbu Fuka, Matcha-Genmaicha, Kukicha, Houjicha), GREEN KISS (Drops, Chews), etc.
ADDRESS: Heeder Dorfstrasse 101, 49356 Diepholz, Germany
TEL: +49-(0)5441-984144
FAX: +49-(0)5441-984145
E-MAIL: shimodozono@t-online.de
WEB: N/A
DISTRIBUTION: Contact company directly

The KEIKO brand brings you a collection of unusually high quality green teas picked at different stages of maturity. KEIKO teas are grown in the region of Kagoshima in Southern Japan, in specially-designed tea yards. Covered with nets (Kabuse) which create a half-shade, they simulate the ideal natural conditions of the wild tea plant. Kabuse-cha is high in nutrients

and has a distinctive fresh taste and aromatic scent. All teas are produced using "CERTIFIED" organic cultivation. Beside Kabuse-cha KEIKO offers Matcha, specialties such as Matcha-Genmaicha, Kukicha, Houjicha and GREEN KISS sweets as well as original Japanese teapots and cups.

Takaokaya U.S.A., Inc.

PRODUCT(S): Aracha, Macha iri genmaicha, Sencha, Kukicha
DISTRIBUTION: Tazaki Foods ☞See p.74

Ujinotsuyuseicha Co., Ltd.

PRODUCT(S): Sencha,Tea bag (Sencha, Houjicha, Genmaicha)
DISTRIBUTION: Harro Foods ☞See p.74

Yamakaen

PRODUCT(S): Macha can
DISTRIBUTION: JFC UK ☞See p.74

YAMA*MOTO*YAMA of America

PRODUCT(S): Tea bags, Loose tea (Green tea, Roasted tea, Brown rice tea, Jasmine tea), Sushi bar style tea (Fukamushi sen-cha, Fukamushi kona-cha)
ADDRESS: Unit 3, 1000 North Circular Rd. London NW2 7JP UK
TEL: +44-(0)20-8452-8883
FAX: +44-(0)20-8452-8883
E-MAIL: kiyoshi@yamamotoyama.freeserve.co.uk
WEB: http://www.yamamotoyama.com
DISTRIBUTION: JFC UK ☞See p.74

As well as being a wonderfully refreshing beverage, Green tea contains many important health components such as catechins, vitamins C and E. YAMA*MOTO*YAMA, with its rich history as a leading green tea merchant since 1690, offers its consumers a wide range of teas carefully blended in both loose leaf and convenient tea bags. In addition to its ever popular traditional green tea products, YAMA*MOTO*YAMA has its very own select blend of bulk Deep-steamed Green (Sencha) tea and Sushi bar style powdered (Konacha) tea. YAMA*MOTO*YAMA with your better health in mind additionally has brand new lines of certified organic and decaffeinated green teas.

Ocha Inryo
Tea Drinks

Asahi Soft Drinks Co., Ltd.

PRODUCT(S): Jurokucha, Oolong tea
DISTRIBUTION: Harro Foods, JFC UK, Tazaki Foods ☞See p.74

Itoen Ltd.

PRODUCT(S): Oh~i ocha, Tennen mineral mugicha
DISTRIBUTION: Harro Foods, JFC UK, Tazaki Foods ☞See p.74

Kirin Brewery Co., Ltd.

PRODUCT(S): Nama cha, Gogo no kocha petbottle (Plain, Milk tea, Lemon tea), Gogo no kocha can (Plain, Milk tea, Lemon tea)
DISTRIBUTION: Harro Foods, JFC UK, Tazaki Foods ☞See p.74

Pokka Corporation

PRODUCT(S): Oolong tea petbottle
DISTRIBUTION: JFC UK ☞See p.74

Suntory Ltd.

PRODUCT(S): Ryokusui, Oolong tea petbottle
DISTRIBUTION: Harro Foods, JFC UK, Tazaki Foods ☞See p.74

Seiryo Inryo
Soft Drinks

Calpis Co., Ltd.

PRODUCT(S): Calpis water (Soft drink can), Calpico soft drink
DISTRIBUTION: Harro Foods, JFC UK, Tazaki Foods ☞See p.74

Japan Tobacco Inc.

PRODUCT(S): Sakuranbo no tennen sui, Momo no tennen sui petbottle
DISTRIBUTION: Harro Foods, JFC UK, Tazaki Foods ☞See p.74

Kenko Inryo
Health Drinks

Otsuka Pharmaceutical Co., Ltd.

PRODUCT(S): Oronamin C, Pokari suetto
DISTRIBUTION: Harro Foods, Tazaki Foods ☞See p.74

Taisho Pharmaceutical (Europe) Ltd.

PRODUCT(S): Lipovitan
ADDRESS: 6-8 Long Lane, London EC1A 9HF UK
TEL: +44-(0)20-7726-8621
FAX: +44-(0)20-7726-8622
E-MAIL: tfujita@taisho.co.uk
WEB: http://www.lipovitan.uk.com
DISTRIBUTION: Contact company directly

Yakult UK Ltd.

PRODUCT(S): Yakult (Fermented milk drinks)
ADDRESS: Westway Estate, 12/16 Telford Way, London W3 7XS UK
TEL: +44-(0)20-8740-4111
FAX: +44-(0)20-8740-4999
E-MAIL: hsuzuki@yakult.co.uk
WEB: http://www.yakult.co.uk
DISTRIBUTION: Contact company directly

NON ALCOHOLIC DRINKS

SOY PRODUCTS

Shoyu
Soy Sauce

Kikkoman Trading Europe GmbH

PRODUCT(S): Naturally Brewed Soy Sauce (original, sweet), Teriyaki Marinade, Sukiyaki Sauce
ADDRESS: Unit 3, 1000 North Circular Rd. Staples Corner, London NW2 7JP UK
TEL: +44-(0)20-8452-8757
FAX: +44-(0)20-8452-4885
E-MAIL: lee@kte.co.uk
WEB: http://www.kikkoman.com
DISTRIBUTION: JFC UK ☞See p.74

KIKKOMAN Soy Sauce is renowned in Japan as a seasoning agent, and has been used there for centuries. Like fine wine, KIKKOMAN Soy Sauce is naturally brewed and fermented. This reddish-brown aromatic seasoning can be used as a table-top condiment as well as a cooking ingredient. KIKKOMAN Sweet Soy Sauce is sweeter and less salty than the original Soy Sauce and provides a subtle accompaniment to all cooked meats, fish and salads. KIKKOMAN Teriyaki Marinade is an authentic Japanese recipe that complements barbecued, grilled, roasted or fried food. KIKKOMAN Sukiyaki Sauce is the ideal sauce for stir-fries with meat, vegetables and noodles.

The Speciality Sauce Company Ltd.

PRODUCT(S): Shoda soysauce (Standard, Superior, Non-GMO, Fish shaped tarebin), The Speciality Sauce company (Organic Japanese soysauce standard, superior, Yakitori sauce)
ADDRESS: 19 Rising Sun Industrial Estate, Blaina, Abertillery, South Wales NP13 3JW UK
TEL: +44-(0)1495-290393
FAX: +44-(0)1495-291831
E-MAIL: toshio.shoda@btinternet.com
WEB: http://www.specialitysauce.co.uk
DISTRIBUTION: Contact company directly, Tazaki Foods ☞See p.74

The Speciality Sauce Company became a subsidiary company of Shoda Shoyu in 1999 and has since sold its products to professional users throughout Europe. The company's main product, shoyu (soy sauce) is an all-purpose sauce suited to both oriental and European dishes. Its biggest seller is an 18 litre pack for restaurateurs but individual portions of shoyu

come in fish-shaped packages and sachets for catering services and lunch boxes. The UK factory also brews an Organic shoyu made from Organic soybeans (Non-GM). Apart from shoyu, the company produces Japanese-style sauces for Yakitori (grilled chicken) and Teriyaki, adapted to the needs of its customers.

Yamasa Corporation

PRODUCT(S): Japanese soy sauce, Sushi shoyu, Less salt soy sauce, Teriyaki sauce, Tsuyu, Sukiyaki sauce, Tairyo dashi, etc.
ADDRESS: 1-23-8 Nihonbashi-Kakigara-cho, Chuo-ku, Tokyo 103-0014 Japan
TEL: +81-(0)3-3668-3366
FAX: +81-(0)3-3668-3177
E-MAIL: intl@yamasa.com
WEB: http://www.yamasa.com/english
DISTRIBUTION: Contact company directly

An uncompromising commitment to quality and tradition has made Yamasa one of Japan's leading manufacturers of soy sauce and the preferred soy sauce of 70% of Tokyo's leading Chefs. Yamasa began its history of soy sauce brewing in1645 and the secret of its success is its use of 100% natural ingredients and traditional production methods. The consistent high quality of Yamasa soy sauce led to increased demand worldwide and an expansion into overseas markets. Free from all artificial ingredients, such as the chemicals DCP and 3MCPD, Yamasa is the naturally brewed soy sauce many consider to be the finest in the world.

Yamato Soysauce & Miso Co., Ltd.

PRODUCT(S): Raw soy sauce, Ponzu, Tamari, Miso, Wasabi, Sushi vinegar, Gari (Pickled ginger), Nori, Udon, Soba
ADDRESS: 4-i-170 Onomachi, Kanazawa-shi, Ishikawa 920-0331 Japan
TEL: +81-(0)76-268-1248
FAX: +81-(0)76-268-1242
E-MAIL: info@yamato-soysauce-miso.co.jp
WEB: http://www.yamato-soysauce-miso.co.jp
DISTRIBUTION: Contact company directly

Founded in 1911, Yamato Soysauce & Miso Co., Ltd. is famed for producing a range of high quality products including shoyu (soy sauce),

miso (fermented soy paste) using only the finest natural ingredients with no artificial additives or flavourings. Yamato also offers all the ingredients necessary for making sushi. Yamato's miso paste and soy sauce are made from high-quality organic soy beans and given a slow natural fermentation process, giving it a unique savoury flavour. Yamato Soysauce & Miso Co., Ltd. produces one of the finest ingredients to make the very best Japanese cuisine and sushi.

Tamari
Tamari Soy Sauce

Clearspring Ltd.

PRODUCT(S): Organic mansan tamari (Double strength)
DISTRIBUTION: Contact company directly ☞See p.71

Sekigahara Jozo

PRODUCT(S): Tamari shoyu
DISTRIBUTION: Harro Foods, JFC UK, Tazaki Foods ☞See p.74

Miso
Fermented Soy Bean Paste

Hanamaruki Foods Inc.

PRODUCT(S): Fuumi-Ichiban, Okaasan
ADDRESS: 4-22-10 Himonya, Meguro-ku, Tokyo 152-8540 Japan
TEL: +81-(0)3-3716-7118
FAX: +81-(0)3-3793-2042
E-MAIL: sasano@hanamaruki.co.jp
WEB: http://www.hanamaruki.co.jp
DISTRIBUTION: Contact company directly

Hanamaruki use only the finest soy beans, cultivated on American and Canadian farms, to make their miso. The HSPS (Hanamaruki Sanitary Production System) is employed to select the best soy beans and rice and strictly administer fermentation, maturation, packing and shipping by machines automatically. Packaging is completed with an automatic filling and packing system that maintains a sterile process with no contact from human hands. Fuumi Ichiban is the delicious end result of the combination of the aromatic, matured miso with carefully selected natural dried bonito flakes and fresh Hokkaido konbu seaweed to create a flavour you can feel.

Ishino Miso

PRODUCT(S): Saikyo miso
DISTRIBUTION: Harro Foods, JFC UK ☞See p.74

Marukome Co., Ltd.

PRODUCT(S): Tokusen miso, Gyomuyo miso shiro, Ryotei no aji cup miso
DISTRIBUTION: Harro Foods, JFC UK, Tazaki Foods ☞See p.74

Maruman Co., Ltd.

PRODUCT(S): Honzukuri shinshu shiro miso, Shinshu honzukuri chukarakuchi
ADDRESS: 2-217 Odori, Iida-shi, Nagano 395-0056 Japan
TEL: +81-(0)726-23-9900
FAX: +81-(0)726-23-9917
E-MAIL: y-kotake@maruman-miso.co.jp
WEB: http://www.maruman-miso.co.jp
DISTRIBUTION: Harro Foods ☞See p.74

Maruman Honzukuri Miso is made from carefully selected high quality ingredients, nurtured in the cleanest air and pure water to create a carefully brewed miso. Honzukuri Shinshu White Miso is a mild and simple style miso. Honzukuri Medium Strength Miso has a fuller, stronger and more traditional flavour. Recent research showed that soybeans, used in good quality, fermented foods like miso, can eliminate the active oxygen which causes various illnesses. It is also thought that soybeans help to prevent aging, high blood pressure, the advancement of cancer and they strengthen bones.

Miyako Oriental Foods, Inc.

PRODUCT(S): Yamajirushi, Yamaizumi, Cold mountain
DISTRIBUTION: Harro Foods ☞See p.74

Miyasaka Brewery Co., Ltd.

PRODUCT(S): Miso (Shiro, Mild, Dashi, Waza shiro), Miso soup (Tofu, Wakame), Instant miso soup (Tofu, Seaweed, Green onion, Fried bean curd)
ADDRESS: 2-4-5 Nogata, Nakano-ku, Tokyo 165-0027 Japan
TEL: +81-(0)3-3385-2121
FAX: +81-(0)3-3387-1366
E-MAIL: m.mukawa@miyasaka-jozo.com
WEB: http://www.miyasaka-jozo.com
DISTRIBUTION: Contact company directly

Miyasaka Brewery Co., Ltd. is the leading manufacture of miso products in Japan. They produce a wide variety of misos, both pastes and easily prepared instant products for retail and industrial use. Their misos compliment meat, fish, and vegetables, and are used widely to flavour fried and grilled dishes as well as in salad dressings. Miyasaka's range of instant soups, which contain ingredients such as wakame (seaweed) and tofu, includes a standard miso soup with a deliciously rich aroma and soups without MSG, all of which can be easily prepared simply by adding hot water.

Yamato Soysauce & Miso Co., Ltd.

PRODUCT(S): Kurodashi nama koji miso, Kanae (Organic rice miso), Yamato nama ginjo miso
DISTRIBUTION: Contact company directly ☞See p.60

Tofu
Soy Bean Curd

G Costa & Co Ltd.

PRODUCT(S): Blue Dragon Firm Silken Style Tofu
ADDRESS: Unit 6, Quarrywood Industrial Estate, Mills Rd. Aylesford, Kent ME20 7NA UK
TEL: +44-(0)1622-713300
FAX: +44-(0)1622-713301
E-MAIL: N/A
WEB: http://www.gcosta.co.uk
DISTRIBUTION: Contact company directly

Blue Dragon has now added Firm Silken Style Tofu to its comprehensive Japanese range. Made with natural soy beans, Blue Dragon Tofu is a source of complete protein and is low in fat. Modern packaging techniques ensure a long life product and mean that freshness is guaranteed. Blue Dragon Tofu's neutral flavour and firm texture make it a highly versatile ingredient, taking on the flavour of any dish it is added to. It is truly the ultimate Japanese cooking ingredient, ideal in a huge range of dishes including stir-fries, soups, salads and casseroles.

House Foods Corporation

PRODUCT(S): Hon-tofu (Tofu powder)
DISTRIBUTION: Harro Foods, JFC UK, Tazaki Foods ☞See p.74

Morinaga Nutritional Foods, Inc.

PRODUCT(S): Silken tofu in tetra pack
DISTRIBUTION: Tazaki Foods ☞See p.74

Tokyo Foods Ltd.

PRODUCT(S): Tokyo tofu
ADDRESS: Unit 10, Artesian Close, Brentfield Rd. London NW10 8RW UK
TEL: +44-(0)20-8830-1942
FAX: +44-(0)20-8830-3696
E-MAIL: N/A
WEB: http://www.japanesetofu.co.uk
DISTRIBUTION: Contact company directly

Inari/Abura Age
Fried Bean Curd

Misuzu-Corporation Co., Ltd.

PRODUCT(S): Flavoured fried tofu pockets, Fried tofu
DISTRIBUTION: Harro Foods, Tazaki Foods ☞See p.74

Yamato

PRODUCT(S): Aburaage, Aburaage gyomuyo, Aji-inari
DISTRIBUTION: JFC UK ☞See p.74

Natto
Fermented Soy Beans

Tokyo Maruju Shokuhin

PRODUCT(S): Hikiwari natto
DISTRIBUTION: JFC UK ☞See p.74

Edamame
Japanese Green Beans

Tsukiji Suisan

PRODUCT(S): Edamame (Boiled green beans - frozen)
DISTRIBUTION: Harro Foods ☞See p.74

Daizu
Soy Beans

Mame no Goto

PRODUCT(S): Tsurunoko daizu
DISTRIBUTION: Harro Foods ☞See p.74

Azuki
Red Beans

Mame no Goto

PRODUCT(S): Azuki (Dried red beans)
DISTRIBUTION: Harro Foods ☞See p.74

Goma
Sesame Seeds

Maruhon

PRODUCT(S): Roasted sesame (White, Black)
DISTRIBUTION: Harro Foods ☞See p.74

TASTE THE DIFFERENCE

"The delicate flavour of Mitsukan's rice vinegar has been carefully developed to bring you a healthier, tasty addition to your meal. Mitsukan, Japan's No.1 rice vinegar in retail and catering sizes."

Tempura Abura
Tempura Oil

Mutual Trading Co., Inc.

PRODUCT(S): Miyako tempra oil
DISTRIBUTION: Harro Foods ☞See p.74

Goma Abura
Sesame Oil

Clearspring Ltd.

PRODUCT(S): Toasted sesame oil
DISTRIBUTION: Contact company directly ☞See p.71

Kadoya

PRODUCT(S): Sesame oil for export
DISTRIBUTION: Harro Foods, Tazaki Foods ☞See p.74

Osu
Japanese Vinegar

Marukan Vinegar (U.S.A.), Inc.

PRODUCT(S): Rice vinegar, Sushi vinegar, Lite rice vinegar, Ginsho rice vinegar, Misho vinegar
ADDRESS: 7755 E.Monroe St. Paramount, CA 90723 USA
TEL: +1-562-602-8340
FAX: +1-562-630-0890
E-MAIL: N/A
WEB: http://www.marukan-usa.com
DISTRIBUTION: JFC UK ☞See p.74

Marukan Vinegar (U.S.A.) Inc. has been producing premium high quality vinegars since 1649. Their slow and natural brewing method is a benchmark of true quality. Their attention to detail guarantees that only the finest vinegars are produced for each of their lines. The Seasoned Gourmet Rice Vinegar, for example, is a top-quality salad vinegar created especially for the gourmet. In November 2002, Marukan Vinegar acquired HACCP (Hazard Analysis and Critical Control Point) certification for the sole purpose of guaranteeing healthy and safe products for their health conscious consumers. Marukan is consistent in producing only the highest quality products.

Nakano Europe Ltd.

PRODUCT(S): Mitsukan (Rice vinegar, Seasoned rice vinegar, Sushi seasoning JS-47
ADDRESS: New Rd. Burntwood, Staffordshire WS7 0AB UK
TEL: +44-(0)154-368-5555

FAX: +44-(0)154-367-7149
E-MAIL: iwabuchi@mitsukan.co.jp **WEB:** N/A
DISTRIBUTION: Contact company directly

The founder of Mitsukan, Matazaemon Nakano, first sold his rice vinegar to merchants in Tokyo nearly 200 years ago. It is now the largest vinegar producer in the world. Mitsukan Rice Vinegar 250ml, 'light and mild', replaces malt, wine or cider vinegar in any of your favourite recipes. It makes food taste even better. Also the 'light and tangy' taste of Seasoned Rice Vinegar 250ml, the number one choice in Japan, can make any dish special. Add zest and flavour to your favourite meals... salads, vegetables, chicken, fish and pasta. Sushi Seasoning JS-47 is already seasoned for sushi rice.

Uchibori Vinegar, Inc.

PRODUCT(S): Pure rice vinegar, Aged spirit vinegar, Seasoned vinegar for sushi
ADDRESS: 437 Igitsushi, Yaotsu-cho, Kamo-gun, Gifu 505-0303 Japan
TEL: +81-(0)574-43-1185
FAX: +81-(0)574-43-1781
E-MAIL: mt.uchibori@uchibori.com
WEB: http://www.uchibori.com
DISTRIBUTION: Contact company directly

Uchibori has been producing rice vinegar for over one hundred years. This sense of tradition calls for the use of all natural ingredients including the finest quality rice and natural spring water in all their vinegar products. The Uchibori range boasts eight different rice vinegars, including organic, brown rice and matured vinegars, as well as a Japanese style dressing. Uchibori vinegars are ideal for use in any number of Japanese and Asian style dishes and are perfect for salad dressings and for fish dishes and sushi. Uchibori is also happy to tailor the flavour of any of its traditionally produced vinegars to meet a specific customer need.

Mirin
Sweet Cooking Sake

Kikkoman Corporation

PRODUCT(S): Manjo hon mirin, Manjo hojun

hon mirin
DISTRIBUTION: JFC UK ☞See p.74

King Jozo

PRODUCT(S): Hinode (Shin miryo, Mirin type seasoning)
DISTRIBUTION: Harro Foods ☞See p.74

Morita Co., Ltd.

PRODUCT(S): Shin mirin, Hon jozo mirin
DISTRIBUTION: Harro Foods ☞See p.74

Nakano Foods Inc.

PRODUCT(S): Mitsukan (Honteri seasoning)
ADDRESS: 55 E. Euclid Ave. Ste. 300, Mt. Prospect, IL 60056 USA
TEL: +1-847-590-0059
FAX: +1-847-590-0484
E-MAIL: N/A **WEB:** N/A
DISTRIBUTION: JFC UK ☞See p.74

Founded in 1804, Mitsukan Group is one of the oldest and largest manufacturers of vinegar in the world. Renowned for its commitment to quality, Mitsukan also produces a range of cooking wines and condiments. Manufactured by its American subsidiary, Nakano Foods Inc., Mitsukan Sweet Mirin Seasoning (also known as Honteri) is non-alcoholic rice based cooking wine used extensively in Asian cuisine. It provides the distinctive flavour of Shabu-Shabu, Sukiyaki and Teriyaki dishes, is a key ingredient in peanut and plum sauces, and a versatile condiment suitable for general cooking.

Ryorishu
Cooking Sake

Kikkoman Corporation

PRODUCT(S): Ryorishu
DISTRIBUTION: JFC UK ☞See p.74

Dashi no Moto
Soup Stocks

Ajinomoto Co., Inc.

PRODUCT(S): Hondashi (Plain, Katsuo, Iriko)
DISTRIBUTION: Harro Foods, JFC UK, Tazaki Foods ☞See p.74

Shimaya Co., Ltd.

PRODUCT(S): Dashi no moto
DISTRIBUTION: Harro Foods, JFC UK, Tazaki Foods ☞See p.74

OILS SEASONINGS

Sosu
Sauces

Bull-Dog Sauce Co., Ltd.

PRODUCT(S): Sauce (Tonkatsu, Chuno, Worcester, Okonomiyaki, Yakisoba)
DISTRIBUTION: Harro Foods, JFC UK, Tazaki Foods ☞See p.74

Ikari Sauce Co., Ltd.

PRODUCT(S): Sauce (Worcester, Tonkatsu, Amakara yakisoba)
DISTRIBUTION: Harro Foods, Tazaki Foods ☞See p.74

Kikkoman Corporation

PRODUCT(S): Sauce (Tonkatsu, Chuno, Worcester)
DISTRIBUTION: JFC UK ☞See p.74

Otafuku Sauce

PRODUCT(S): Okonomiyaki sauce, Yakisoba sauce
DISTRIBUTION: Harro Foods, JFC UK, Tazaki Foods ☞See p.74

Tare
Dipping Sauces

Ebara Foods Co., Ltd.

PRODUCT(S): Tare (Yakiniku, Sukiyaki, Yakitori), Ogon no aji (Hot, Mild, Medium-hot)
DISTRIBUTION: Harro Foods, JFC UK, Tazaki Foods ☞See p.74

Kikkoman Trading Europe GmbH

PRODUCT(S): Teriyaki marinade, Sukiyaki sauce
DISTRIBUTION: Contact company directly ☞See p.60

Mitsukan Group Corporation

PRODUCT(S): Pon shabu, Goma shabu, Gyoza no tare
DISTRIBUTION: Harro Foods, JFC UK, Tazaki Foods ☞See p.74

Nihon Shokken Co., Ltd.

PRODUCT(S): Yakitori tsukekomi tare, Nuttare, Unagi no tare special
ADDRESS: Friedrich-Ebert, Str. 17 40210 Duesseldorf, Germany
TEL: +49-(0)211-499-751
FAX: +49-(0)211-498-313
E-MAIL: nsgermany@kddnet.de
WEB: http://nihonshokken.co.jp
DISTRIBUTION: Tazaki Foods ☞See p.74

Doresshingu
Salad Dressings

Mitsukan Group Corporation

PRODUCT(S): Dressing (Soy sauce, Yuzu, Goma, Chinese)
DISTRIBUTION: Harro Foods, JFC UK, Tazaki Foods ☞See p.74

Tsuyu
Noodle Soup Stocks

Kikkoman Corporation

PRODUCT(S): Menmi, Hon tsuyu, Tsuyu (Somen, Zaru soba, Zaru udon, Ume katsuo)
ADDRESS: 2-1-1 Nishi-Shinbashi, Minato-ku, Tokyo 105-8428 Japan
TEL: +81-(0)3-5521-5365
FAX: +81-(0)3-5521-5369
E-MAIL: N/A
WEB: http://www.kikkoman.co.jp
DISTRIBUTION: JFC UK ☞See p.74

Kikkoman's Hon Tsuyu, concentrated stock for Japanese noodle soup, is produced as the basis for all sorts of Japanese noodle dishes. Made from natural bonito and kelp stocks and high quality soy sauce, Hon Tsuyu is perfect for use in soba and udon noodle meals, as well as hot pot and other boiled dishes. The Increased quantity of bonito and kelp stocks in each pack has made it even more enjoyable. As Hon Tsuyu is concentrated at three times the thickness of the standard amount, you can adjust the taste as you like. Kikkoman's famous product is available in one litre packs, or 500ml bottles.

Ninben

PRODUCT(S): Tsuyu, Tsuyu no moto
DISTRIBUTION: Harro Foods, JFC UK, Tazaki Foods ☞See p.74

Yamasa Corporation

PRODUCT(S): Konbu tsuyu, Tsuyu (Soba, Udon, Somen, Tempura)
DISTRIBUTION: Harro Foods, Tazaki Foods ☞See p.74

Wasabi
Japanese Horseradish

House Foods Corporation

PRODUCT(S): Wasabiko, Wasabi paste in tube
DISTRIBUTION: Harro Foods, JFC UK, Tazaki Foods ☞See p.74

Kaneku Co., Ltd.

PRODUCT(S): Tokusen oroshi nama wasabi, 150 Honnama wasabi, Kona wasabi green, Neriume siso, Reito kizami namayuzu, GMO-Free kona wasabi
ADDRESS: 1-12-19 Minamihorie, Nishi-ku, Osaka-shi 550-0015 Japan

TEL: +81-(0)6-6531-4332
FAX: +81-(0)6-6543-4300
E-MAIL: 0135shimizu@kaneku-wasabi.co.jp
WEB: http://www.kaneku-wasabi.co.jp
DISTRIBUTION: Harro Foods ☞See p.74

Wasabi, the Japanese horseradish with a pungent flavour, is best known to western diners as an accompaniment to sushi and sashimi. Having started as a small family business in 1927, Kaneku Co., Ltd. then became one of the largest producers of wasabi in Japan. Marrying decades-old tradition with cutting edge modern technology, Kaneku's top quality wasabi powder and paste is now produced at a new state of the art factory in Shimane prefecture, offering unparalleled levels of hygiene and quality control. Kaneku still retains its passionate commitment to producing the best possible wasabi.

SB Foods Inc.

PRODUCT(S): Wasabi paste in tube
DISTRIBUTION: Harro Foods, JFC UK, Tazaki Foods ☞See p.74

Tokyo Kaneku Co., Ltd.

PRODUCT(S): Kona wasabi, Neri wasabi, Gari, Amazu shoga
ADDRESS: Kaneku Bldg. 3-27-11 Yushima, Bunkyo-ku, Tokyo 113-0034 Japan
TEL: +81-(0)3-3831-1688
FAX: +81-(0)3-3836-9067
E-MAIL: michiko1514@aol.com
WEB: N/A
DISTRIBUTION: JFC UK ☞See p.74

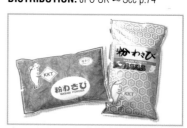

Tokyo Kaneku Co., Ltd. is a manufacturer of powdered wasabi, the Japanese horseradish, which is a crucial seasoning for sushi and sashimi. Tokyo Kaneku's powdered wasabi only needs added cold water and sufficient kneading before it is ready to serve. As well as its traditional use as an accompaniment to sushi and sashimi, Tokyo Kaneku's powdered wasabi can be used in a variety of ways: as an ingredient in salad dressing or mayonnaise for example. Tokyo Kaneku produces its powdered wasabi in cans decorated with Ukiyoe pictures (Japanese traditional wood block prints).

Waner Incorporated

PRODUCT(S): Kinjirushi wasabi
ADDRESS: 3-11-6 Tsukiji, Chuo-ku, Tokyo 104-0045 Japan
TEL: +81-(0)3-3541-1591
FAX: +81-(0)3-3541-4150
E-MAIL: w-uchida@kinjirushi.co.jp
WEB: http://www.kinjirushi.co.jp
DISTRIBUTION: Contact company directly

Karashi
Mustard/Chilli Pepper

House Foods Corporation

PRODUCT(S): Karashiko (Mustard powder)
DISTRIBUTION: Harro Foods, JFC UK, Tazaki Foods ☞See p.74

SB Foods Inc.

PRODUCT(S): Karashiko, Mustard paste in tube
DISTRIBUTION: Harro Foods, JFC UK, Tazaki Foods ☞See p.74

Katsuobushi
Bonito Flakes

JFC (UK) Ltd.

PRODUCT(S): Hanakatsuo
DISTRIBUTION: JFC UK ☞See p.74

Nori
Nori Seaweed

Shirako Co., Ltd.

PRODUCT(S): Okazu nori, Choshoku ajinori, Yakisushi nori (Gold, Silver), Kizaminori
DISTRIBUTION: Harro Foods, JFC UK ☞See p.74

Tokyo Nagai Co., Ltd.

PRODUCT(S): Roasted seaweed, Roasted seaweed Honasakusa, Seasoned seaweed, Teriyakinori, Okazunori, Kagayaki
ADDRESS: 3-2-10 Omorinaka, Ota-ku, Tokyo 143-0014 Japan
TEL: +81-(0)3-3764-5621
FAX: +81-(0)3-3764-5625
E-MAIL: nagainr@attglobal.net
WEB: N/A
DISTRIBUTION: JFC UK ☞See p.74

Tokyo Nagai's roasted nori seaweed has been carefully selected for its excellence in sushi rolls, its pleasant aroma and deliciously crisp texture. It is available in many different types that vary according to grade and usage. In this way, Tokyo Nagai creates nori products which can satisfy even the most discerning customers. The superb quality of the seaweed is ensured through careful automatic and computerised selection, along with metal detection and the usage of sterile receptacles. Today this precise system is employed in a hygienic and HACCP-compliant environment to bring customers nori seaweed of the very highest quality.

Urashima USA., Inc

PRODUCT(S): Urashima nori
ADDRESS: 307 Paseo Sonrisa, Walnut, CA 91789 USA
TEL: +1-909-869-5946
FAX: +1-909-869-0565
E-MAIL: info@urashimausa.com
WEB: http://www.urashimausa.com
DISTRIBUTION: Harro Foods ☞See p.74

Urashima Nori has been producing and processing nori seaweed in Japan since 1914. Crisp in texture with a distinctive flavour, nori has always been a popular food in East Asia and is an essential ingredient in Sushi. It has become increasingly popular in the USA and in European countries as it is a rich source of essential minerals, including calcium, phosphorous, iron and zinc. Building on its reputation for quality, Urashima nori has expanded into the Chinese and Taiwanese markets and has now successfully established itself as a leading producer and distributor of finest nori seaweed in America and Europe.

YAMA*MOTO*YAMA of America

PRODUCT(S): Yaki sushi nori, Teriyaki nori, Onigiri wrap (Rice ball nori)
ADDRESS: Unit 3, 1000 North Circular Rd. London NW2 7JP UK
TEL: +44-(0)20-8452-8883
FAX: +44-(0)20-8452-8883
E-MAIL: kiyoshi@yamamotoyama.freeserve.co.uk
WEB: http://www.yamamotoyama.com
DISTRIBUTION: JFC UK ☞See p.74

Nori (seaweed) is a valuable nutritional source filled with vitamins and minerals. Nori is an essential ingredient in many Japanese dishes such as Maki-Sushi (rolled sushi), Onigiri (rice ball), topping for noodles and salads etc.... YAMA*MOTO*YAMA, since 1947, has long been recognized as one of the premier manufacturers of roasted seaweed. YAMA*MOTO*YAMA of America, an US subsidiary established in 1975, has been introducing a wide range of seaweed such as roasted sushi nori, roll nori (for sushi machine), seasoned nori (teriyaki, hot, wasabi, aojiso flavours), shredded nori and kosher certified nori to the consumers on a world wide basis.

Aonori
Green Seaweed Flakes

Mishima

PRODUCT(S): Aonoriko (Seaweed powder)
DISTRIBUTION: JFC UK, Tazaki Foods ☞See p.74

Wakame
Wakame Seaweed

Riken Vitamin Co., Ltd.

PRODUCT(S): Wakame hanazaiku, Fueru wakame, Cut wakame
DISTRIBUTION: Harro Foods, JFC UK, Tazaki Foods ☞See p.74

Konbu
Kelp

Otomegusa

PRODUCT(S): Hidaka konbu
DISTRIBUTION: Harro Foods ☞See p.74

Yokoi Konbu

PRODUCT(S): Tashiro dashi konbu
DISTRIBUTION: Harro Foods ☞See p.74

Hijiki
Hijiki Seaweed

Otomegusa

PRODUCT(S): Mehijiki (Dried seaweed)
DISTRIBUTION: Harro Foods ☞See p.74

Tomen Foods UK Ltd.

PRODUCT(S): Hijiki
DISTRIBUTION: Contact company directly ☞See p.53

Hoshi Shiitake
Dried Mushroom

Shinkan

PRODUCT(S): Dried shiitake mushroom
DISTRIBUTION: Harro Foods ☞See p.74

SPICES/SEAWEEDS MUSHROOMS

65

Beni Shoga/Gari
Red/Pickled Ginger

Tokyo Kaneku Co., Ltd.

PRODUCT(S): Amasu shoga pink
DISTRIBUTION: JFC UK, Tazaki Foods ☞See p.74

Umeboshi
Pickled Plums

Clearspring Ltd.

PRODUCT(S): Organic umeboshi plums, Umeboshi puree
DISTRIBUTION: Contact company directly ☞See p.71

Tsukemono
Japanese Pickles

Shin-Shin Foods Co., Ltd.

PRODUCT(S): Yama gobo zuke, Shibazuke, Ao shisonori, Koume zuke, Ninniku tamarizuke, Tokusen parikyu, Sakurazuke, Fukujinzuke, Beni shoga, Parikko, Shichimi zasai, Bibinba sansai, Ninniku misozuke
DISTRIBUTION: Harro Foods, JFC UK, Tazaki Foods ☞See p.74

Tokai Tsukemono Seizo

PRODUCT(S): Shibori takuwan, Takuwan taro, Tokyo takuwan, Shibazuke kyoyukari
DISTRIBUTION: Harro Foods, JFC UK, Tazaki Foods ☞See p.74

Konnyaku/Shirataki
Konnyaku Jelly

Tsuruta Shokuhin Chiba

PRODUCT(S): Mutsumi (Ita konnyaku shiro & kuro, Shirataki, Jumbo shirataki)
DISTRIBUTION: Harro Foods, JFC UK, Tazaki Foods ☞See p.74

Udon
Wheat Noodles

Fukui Seimen

PRODUCT(S): Soba, Udon, Ramen
ADDRESS: 3-715 Tonya, Fukui-shi, Fukui 918-8231 Japan
TEL: +81-(0)776-21-4477
FAX: +81-(0)776-21-4475
E-MAIL: info@mentaiya.co.jp
WEB: http://www.mentaiya.co.jp
DISTRIBUTION: Contact company directly

Myojo U.S.A., Inc.

PRODUCT(S): Fresh udon with soup (Beef, Chicken, Mushroom, Oriental, Shrimp), Fresh jumbo udon with soup, Fresh udon no soup

ADDRESS: 6220 Prescott Ct. Chino CA 91710 USA
TEL: +1-909-464-1411
FAX: +1-909-464-1415
E-MAIL: naka185@attglobal.net **WEB:** N/A
DISTRIBUTION: JFC UK ☞See p.74

Founded in California in 1991 as a subsidiary company of Myojo Foods Japan and JFC International, Myojo U.S.A., Inc. has introduced Myojo products to US and European markets using the extensive JFC distribution network. The company makes a variety of Japanese style noodles like udon, stir fry noodles (yakisoba) and ramen, as well as the dough used in the skins of gyoza, Japanese dumplings. Myojo has been popular and successful in the Japanese domestic market and the Asian food market in the USA for years. Myojo is now establishing its reputation for quality and authenticity in the British and European markets.

Nagai Syokuhin

PRODUCT(S): Sanuki udon
DISTRIBUTION: Harro Foods, JFC UK ☞See p.74

Sanshu

PRODUCT(S): Honba sanuki udon
DISTRIBUTION: Harro Foods ☞See p.74

Yousuke Satou of the 7th Generations

PRODUCT(S): Inaniwa udon
ADDRESS: 229 Inaniwa, Inakawa-machi, Ogachi-gun, Akita 012-0169 Japan
TEL: +81-(0)183-43-2226 (Japanese only)
FAX: +81-(0)183-43-2812
E-MAIL: yosukeji@yutopia.or.jp
WEB: http://www.inaniwa-udon.co.jp
DISTRIBUTION: Contact company directly

It could be said that the history of Yousuke Satou of the 7th Generation is that of Inaniwa dry udon itself. Renowned for their unique flavour and digestibility, Inaniwa dry udon has been immensely popular since Yousuke Satou started producing them in 1860. Made by craftsmen from only flour, salt and clear water, Inaniwa dry udon differs significantly from conventionally produced udon. Once mixed, the dough is left for 24 hours before being spun by hand and left to dry naturally. This traditional approach results in a flavour and quality impossible to produce by machine and makes Inaniwa among the finest udon available.

Soba
Buckwheat Noodles

Aoi

PRODUCT(S): Nihon soba
DISTRIBUTION: JFC UK ☞See p.74

Ikeda Seimen

PRODUCT(S): Zaohkogen soba
DISTRIBUTION: JFC UK ☞See p.74

Ishiguro Seimen

PRODUCT(S): Yamaimo soba
DISTRIBUTION: Harro Foods, JFC UK, Tazaki Foods ☞See p.74

Miura Shokuhin

PRODUCT(S): Zao soba
DISTRIBUTION: Harro Foods ☞See p.74

Nisshin Foods Inc.

PRODUCT(S): Shinsyu soba
DISTRIBUTION: JFC UK ☞See p.74

Shigeno

PRODUCT(S): Zaru soba
DISTRIBUTION: JFC UK ☞See p.74

Yamagata Asahi Soba

PRODUCT(S): Asahi soba, Asahi chasoba
DISTRIBUTION: Harro Foods ☞See p.74

Somen/Hiyamugi
Thin Wheat Noodles

Nisshin Foods Inc.

PRODUCT(S): No.1 somen, No.1 hiyamugi
DISTRIBUTION: Harro Foods, JFC UK, Tazaki Foods ☞See p.74

Sokuseki Men
Instant Noodles

Myojo Foods Co., Ltd.

PRODUCT(S): Chuka zanmai (Kanton, Peking, Shisen, Reimen), Chukamen gyomuyo, Ippei chan (Shoyu, Kokumiso, Koku tonkotsu, Yakisoba)
DISTRIBUTION: Harro Foods, JFC UK ☞See p.74

Nissin Food Products Co., Ltd.

PRODUCT(S): Cup noodle (Plain, Curry, Cheese curry, Seafood, Seafood yakisoba), Raoh (Shoyu,

Miso, Tonkotsu cup), Men no tatsujin (Shoyu, Tonkotsu, Shoyu tonkotsu, Miso tonkotsu, Shoyu Cup), Men no shokunin (Miso, Shio tanmen), Ramenyasan (Asahikawa shoyu, Sapporo miso)
DISTRIBUTION: Harro Foods, JFC UK, Tazaki Foods ☞See p.74

Nissin Foods GmbH Europe

PRODUCT(S): Demae ramen, Cup noodles
ADDRESS: Am Hohenstein 3-5, 65779 Kelkheim, Germany
TEL: +49-(0)6195-6927
FAX: +49-(0)6195-910019
E-MAIL: KazuhitoKusumoto@nissin-foods.de
WEB: http://www.nissinfoods.co.jp/english
DISTRIBUTION: Contact company directly

Sanyo Foods Corporation of America

PRODUCT(S): Sapporo ichiban (Original, Miso, Shrimp, Chicken, Beef)
DISTRIBUTION: JFC UK, Tazaki Foods ☞See p.74

Toyo Suisan Co., Ltd.

PRODUCT(S): Maruchan: Akai kitsune, Midori no tanuki, Dekamaru (Corn butter, Moyashi miso), Cup menzukuri shoyu, Hiyashi ramen (Regular, Goma)
DISTRIBUTION: Harro Foods, JFC UK ☞See p.74

Sokuseki Misoshiru
Instant Miso Soup

Hanamaruki Foods Inc.

PRODUCT(S): Miso soup (Aka, Shiro, Tofu, Ume), Osuimono
DISTRIBUTION: Contact company directly ☞See p.60

Kikkoman Corporation

PRODUCT(S): Misoshiru (Aka, Shiro, Tofu, Horenso), Wakame soup, Osuimono
DISTRIBUTION: JFC UK ☞See p.74

Miyasaka Brewery Co., Ltd.

PRODUCT(S): Instant miso soup (Tofu, Seaweed, Green onion, Fried bean curd)
DISTRIBUTION: Contact company directly ☞See p.61

Nagatanien

PRODUCT(S): Miso soup (Asage, Hiruge, Yuuge), Matsutake osuimono
DISTRIBUTION: Harro Foods, JFC UK, Tazaki Foods ☞See p.74

Sokuseki Gohan
Instant Rice

Sato Foods Industries Co., Ltd.

PRODUCT(S): Koshihikari cooked rice
DISTRIBUTION: Harro Foods, JFC UK ☞See p.74

Furikake
Toppings for Rice

Marumiya Foods

PRODUCT(S): Noritama
DISTRIBUTION: Harro Foods, JFC UK, Tazaki Foods ☞See p.74

Nagatanien

PRODUCT(S): Otona no furikake (Katsuo, Wasabi)
DISTRIBUTION: Harro Foods, JFC UK, Tazaki Foods ☞See p.74

Kare
Curry

House Foods Corporation

PRODUCT(S): Vermont curry (Hot, Medium hot, Mild), Java curry (Hot, Medium hot, Mild, Gyomuyo), Kokumaro curry (Hot, Medium hot, Mild)
DISTRIBUTION: Harro Foods, JFC UK, Tazaki Foods ☞See p.74

SB Foods Inc.

PRODUCT(S): Golden curry roux, Golden curry (Hot, Medium hot, Mild), Torokeru curry (Hot, Medium hot, Mild)
DISTRIBUTION: Harro Foods, JFC UK, Tazaki Foods ☞See p.74

Sokuseki ~ no Moto
Seasoning Mixes

Ebara Foods Co., Ltd.

PRODUCT(S): Asazuke no moto (Plain, Shiso ume)
DISTRIBUTION: Harro Foods, JFC UK, Tazaki Foods ☞See p.74

Marumiya Foods

PRODUCT(S): Kamameshi no moto (Shake, Kinoko, Matsutake)
DISTRIBUTION: Harro Foods, JFC UK, Tazaki Foods ☞See p.74

Mitsukan Group Corporation

PRODUCT(S): Gomoku chirashi no moto
DISTRIBUTION: Harro Foods, JFC UK, Tazaki Foods ☞See p.74

Momoya Co., Ltd.

PRODUCT(S): Kimuchi no moto
DISTRIBUTION: Harro Foods, JFC UK, Tazaki Foods ☞See p.74

Nagatanien

PRODUCT(S): Ochazuke (Nori, Shake, Tarako), Sushi taro
DISTRIBUTION: Harro Foods, JFC UK, Tazaki Foods ☞See p.74

Tamanoi

PRODUCT(S): Sushi no ko
DISTRIBUTION: Harro Foods, JFC UK, Tazaki Foods ☞See p.74

Tempurako
Tempura Flour

Mutual Trading Co., Inc.

PRODUCT(S): Miyako (Tempura flour mix, New king tempura flour)
DISTRIBUTION: Harro Foods ☞See p.74

Nisshin Foods Inc.

PRODUCT(S): Tempura batter mix, Karaageko, Tatsutaageko
ADDRESS: 1-25 Kanda-Nishiki-cho, Chiyoda-ku, Tokyo 101-8441 Japan
TEL: +81-(0)3-5282-C221
FAX: +81-(0)3-5282-6125
E-MAIL: sasaia@mail.ni-net.co.jp
WEB: http://www.nisshin.com
DISTRIBUTION: JFC UK ☞See p.74

Nisshin Foods Inc. is a core company within the Nisshin Seifun Group, which produces a wide range of both dry and frozen processed food products including flours, premixed sauces and batters and both dried and frozen noodles. One of Nisshin Foods' leading products is its powdered batter for tempura, the Japanese deep-fried dish. When prepared, Nisshin Foods' batter produces a crisp, wonderfully light tempura with a rich, authentically Japanese flavour. As it comes powdered and unseasoned, Nisshin Foods' tempura batter mix is extremely versatile, allowing the chef to season the batter to his or her individual taste.

Panko
Bread Crumbs

Nisshin Foods Inc.

PRODUCT(S): Soft bread crumbs, Panko No. 5
DISTRIBUTION: Harro Foods, JFC UK ☞See p.74

Katakuriko
Potato Starch

Kawamitsu Bussan

PRODUCT(S): Hoshito katakuriko (Starch)
DISTRIBUTION: Harro Foods, Tazaki Foods ☞See p.74

Shiratamako
Shiratama Mix

Kimura

PRODUCT(S): Usagi shiratamako
DISTRIBUTION: JFC UK, Tazaki Foods ☞See p.74

Sushi
Sushi

Budokan Retail Ltd.

PRODUCT(S): Packed sushi
ADDRESS: 31 Colston St. Bristol BS1 5AP UK
TEL: +44-(0)8708-377-311
FAX: +44-(0)8708-377-349
E-MAIL: kwarrick@budokan.co.uk
WEB: http://www.budokan.co.uk/retail
DISTRIBUTION: Contact company directly

Budokan supplies a range of packed sushi to the retail and catering industries. The range includes two pack sizes of 150 gms and 210 gms offering combinations of vegetarian, cooked fish and raw fish sushi. Daily delivery can be made across the south and southwest. Budokan's sushi is currently listed with multiple stores, such as Somerfield and Compass group, along with regional delis and gourmet sandwhich shops. Budokan retail plans to extend the range of packaged meals to include Budokan classics like Thai green and red curry, mee goreng and nasi goreng.

Reito Sushi/Neta
Frozen Sushi/Toppings for Sushi

Harro Foods Ltd.

PRODUCT(S): Harro sushi neta (Sushi ebi, Sliced ika, Sliced tako, Ama ebi, Kanpyo, Sliced shiitake, etc.)
ADDRESS: 23A Lombard Rd. Merton, London SW19 3TZ UK
TEL: +44-(0)20-8543-3343
FAX: +44-(0)20-8542-1962
E-MAIL: ikubo@harro.co.uk
WEB: http://www.harro.co.uk
DISTRIBUTION: Contact company directly

With over 2,000 products, Harro Foods Ltd. supplies major Japanese restaurants, (especially conveyor-belt sushi restaurant chains) airlines, retail shops, hotels and commercial catering contractors. They can also provide you with accurate information on products, markets and suppliers. Harro Foods' sushi toppings include maguro (tuna), ebi (prepared black tiger prawn), ama-ebi (northern pink shrimp), ika (sliced cuttle fish), tako (sliced octopus), ikura (salmon roe), tobikko (flying fish roe), and others. They also supply sushi rice, sushi vinegar, soy sauce, nori seaweed, wasabi, gari (pickled ginger), etc., and drinks such as green tea, oolong tea, sake and shochu.

Kairinmaru Beer Co., Ltd.

PRODUCT(S): Otaru ai no sushi, Otaru jun-jou soba
ADDRESS: 1-8-16 Takashima, Otaru-shi, Hokkaido 047-0048 Japan
TEL: +81-(0)134-33-5623
FAX: +81-(0)134-33-5639
E-MAIL: sea@kairinmaru.net
WEB: http://www.kairinmaru.net
DISTRIBUTION: Contact company directly

Kairinmaru Beer Co., Ltd. produces ready to eat sushi and soba (buckwheat-noodle). Their frozen sushi, which contains no chemical additives, is the most popular variety in Japan, and won first prize at the 2001 Hokkaido Processed Food Fair. Their sushi is also sold in USA and has gained a good reputation. Good quality soba helps to prevent high blood pressure and heart diseases; however, as wheat flour is often added to soba in order to make it sticky, it is quite difficult to find 100% buckwheat soba. Kairinmaru's instant frozen soba is an authentic 100% buckwheat soba. You can prepare by simply pouring hot water over it.

Reito Shokuzai
Frozen Ingredients

Harro Foods Ltd.

PRODUCT(S): Vegetables, Seafood
DISTRIBUTION: Harro Foods ☞See p.74

JFC (UK) Ltd.

PRODUCT(S): Vegetables, Seafood
DISTRIBUTION: JFC UK ☞See p.74

Tazaki Foods Ltd.

PRODUCT(S): Vegetables, Seafood
DISTRIBUTION: Tazaki Foods ☞See p.74

Reito Souzai
Frozen Ready Meals

Hosho Holland B.V.

PRODUCT(S): Kibun (Honzukuri kamaboko aka/shiro, Imitation crab stick, Takebue, Oden no neta, Osechi set, etc.)
ADDRESS: Beurs-World Trade Centre 504, Beursplein 37, P.O. Box 30128, 3001 DC, Rotterdam, Holland
TEL: +31-(0)10-405-6565
FAX: +31-(0)10-405-5170
E-MAIL: Sakamoto@hosho.nl
WEB: N/A
DISTRIBUTION: Harro Foods, JFC UK, Tazaki Foods ☞See p.74

Miyasun Foods Company

PRODUCT(S): Chicken flavoured with sweet vinegar, Steamed chicken, Chicken teriyaki, Japanese-style boiled beef, Chicken nanban (breast), etc.
ADDRESS: 210 Shoei-cho, Miyazaki-shi, Miyazaki 880-0833 Japan
TEL: +81-(0)985-29-2383
FAX: +81-(0)985-29-2384
E-MAIL: k.hiwatashi@miyasun.co.jp
WEB: http://www.miyasun.co.jp
DISTRIBUTION: Contact company directly

Miyasun Foods Company produces and sells frozen meat-based ready meals. With factories in China as well as Japan, the company produces over 9,000 tons of products per year. Most of its customers are professional users in the restaurant and catering trades. As all the products are fully cooked, all the customer has to do is to reheat them in a microwave or a fryer before serving. The company is able to offer new products following recipes given by customers and is able to fine tune the taste and texture of existing products to customers' needs.

Reito Men
Frozen Noodles

Shimadaya Corporation

PRODUCT(S): Nama ramen (Shoyu, Shio, Miso)
DISTRIBUTION: Harro Foods, JFC UK, Tazaki Foods ☞See p.74

Sundelic Foods Co., Ltd.

PRODUCT(S): Meijin udon, Meijin soba
DISTRIBUTION: JFC UK ☞See p.74

Toyo Suisan Co., Ltd.

PRODUCT(S): Maruchan nama yakisoba, Maruchan nama ramen (Shoyu, Miso)
DISTRIBUTION: JFC UK, Tazaki Foods ☞See p.74

SUSHI
FROZEN FOODS

For the best in organic and authentic Japanese foods made to time-honoured recipes by traditional methods.

Clearspring®

Discover more of our award winning range

Senbei/Arare
Rice Crackers

Amanoya Corporation

PRODUCT(S): Kabuki age, Himemaru arare, Otsumami mix
DISTRIBUTION: Harro Foods, JFC UK, Tazaki Foods ☞See p.74

Clearspring Ltd.

PRODUCT(S): Organic rice crackers, Rice cakes
ADDRESS: Sales&Marketing Office, 16-18 Shardlow Rd. Alvaston, Derby DE24 OJH UK
TEL: +44-(0)1332-756622
FAX: +44 (0)1332 233467
E-MAIL: sales@clearspring.co.uk
WEB: http://www.clearspring.co.uk
DISTRIBUTION: Contact company directly

Clearspring's aim is to provide their customers with only the most delicious, wholesome and nutritious foods that are produced by traditional methods that respect the natural environment. Their suppliers are primarily small-scale family producers who are committed to producing the highest quality foods by traditional, time-honoured processing methods. This ensures that the flavour and quality of their foods are always of the highest standards. All Clearspring products are vegan, free from added sugar and contain no artificial additives of any kind. They have a wide range of authentic Japanese products available from seasonings and pickles to noodles and delicious snacks.

Iwatsuka Seika

PRODUCT(S): Hibiyaki, Hyoban yaki, Atsuyaki salad, Mamemochi salad, Macadamia-nuts Okaki, Niigata age shio
DISTRIBUTION: Harro Foods, JFC UK, Tazaki Foods ☞See p.74

Kameda Seika Co., Ltd.

PRODUCT(S): Super fresh kakinotane, Umenoka-maki, Age-ichiban, etc.
ADDRESS: 3-1-1 Kamedakogyo-danchi, Kameda-machi, Nakakanbara-gun, Niigata 950-0198 Japan
TEL: +81-(0)25-382-2111
FAX: +81-(0)25-381-7200
E-MAIL: N/A
WEB: http://www.kamedaseika.co.jp
DISTRIBUTION: Harro Foods ☞See p.74

Kameda Seika produce Super Fresh Kakinotane rice crackers - a best selling favourite in Japan and a versatile treat which can be eaten in many different occasions - as a snack on their own or as something to nibble with beer. Each bag contains six packs.

Umenoka-maki is a popular rice cracker made with delicious plums, baked until beautifully brown and then wrapped in a lightly grilled crisp seaweed sheet. Age-ichiban rice crackers are fried in piping hot oil to create a light and crisp savoury. This tasty snack is then flavoured with a full-bodied soy sauce.

Sunakku
Savoury Snacks

Calbee Foods Co., Ltd.

PRODUCT(S): Kappa ebisen, Osatsu sweet potato, Sapporo potato & vegetable, Shrimp chips
DISTRIBUTION: Harro Foods, JFC UK, Tazaki Foods ☞See p.74

Meiji Seika Kaisha, Ltd.

PRODUCT(S): Curl cheese, Curl usu aji
DISTRIBUTION: Harro Foods, JFC UK, Tazaki Foods ☞See p.74

Tohato Co., Ltd.

PRODUCT(S): Caramel corn, Caramel corn strawberry
DISTRIBUTION: Harro Foods, JFC UK, Tazaki Foods ☞See p.74

Mamegashi
Bean Snacks

Imoto

PRODUCT(S): Wasabi pea
DISTRIBUTION: JFC UK ☞See p.74

Kasugai Seika

PRODUCT(S): Roasted green pea, Usu pea, Green wasabi pea, Ika pea
DISTRIBUTION: Harro Foods, JFC UK ☞See p.74

Karinto
Snacks with Brown Sugar

Kanezaki Seika

PRODUCT(S): Edo fumi karinto (Kuro, Peanut)
DISTRIBUTION: JFC UK, Tazaki Foods ☞See p.74

Chokoreito-gashi
Chocolate Treats

Ezaki Glico Co., Ltd.

PRODUCT(S): Pocky, Caplico stick

DISTRIBUTION: JFC UK, Tazaki Foods ☞See p.74

Lotte Co., Ltd.

PRODUCT(S): Koala no march (Chocolate, Strawberry)
DISTRIBUTION: JFC UK, Tazaki Foods ☞See p.74

Meiji Seika Kaisha, Ltd.

PRODUCT(S): Kinoko no yama, Takenoko no sato
DISTRIBUTION: JFC UK, Tazaki Foods ☞See p.74

Royce Confect Co., Ltd.

PRODUCT(S): Nama chocolate
ADDRESS: 5-11-1 Odori-Nishi, Chuo-ku, Sapporo-shi, Hokkaido 060-8646 Japan
TEL: +81-(0)11-218-1000
FAX: +81-(0)11-218-1113
E-MAIL: overseas3@royce-confect.co.jp
WEB: http://www.e-royce.com
DISTRIBUTION: Contact company directly

Gamu
Chewing Gum

Marukawa Seika

PRODUCT(S): Bubble gum (Orange, Strawberry, Grape)
DISTRIBUTION: JFC UK ☞See p.74

Gumi/Sofuto Candi
Gummy/Chewy Sweets

Kasugai Seika

PRODUCT(S): Gumi 100 (Grape, Apple, Orange, Mix)
DISTRIBUTION: Harro Foods, JFC UK ☞See p.74

Morinaga & Co., Ltd.

PRODUCT(S): Hi-chu (Strawberry, Ao ringo, Grape, Yoghurt)
DISTRIBUTION: JFC UK, Tazaki Foods ☞See p.74

Yokan
Bean Paste Jelly

Murai Syokuhin Kogyosho

PRODUCT(S): Azuma (Kuri yokan, Macha yokan)
DISTRIBUTION: JFC UK ☞See p.74

Yoneya

PRODUCT(S): Mini neri yokan, Mini ogura yokan
DISTRIBUTION: Harro Foods, JFC UK, Tazaki Foods ☞See p.74

Reito Wagashi
Frozen Japanese Cakes

Yoshikawa

PRODUCT(S): Ohagi, Kushi dango, Kashiwa mochi, Sakura mochi, Daifuku
DISTRIBUTION: Tazaki Foods ☞See p.74

SNACKS
CONFECTIONERIES

The **Maki** and **Nigiri** Robots
- making quality **Sushi** Simple!

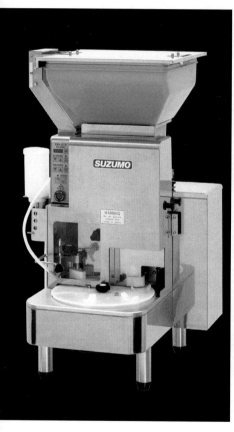

For all your sushi needs contact **SKERMAN PROMAC LTD.**

Tel: +44(0)1932 789646
Fax: +44(0)1932 761830
Email: skermanpromac@skerman.com
162 Windmill Road West Sunbury on Thames TW16 7HB

WE LOVE RICE
SUZUMO

Certified!

Shukanki
Sake Warmers

Taiji & Co., Ltd.

PRODUCT(S): Sake warmer
DISTRIBUTION: Harro Foods, JFC UK, Tazaki Foods ☞See p.74

Gasu Konro/Nabe/Teppan
Cookers/Pans/Hot Plates

Iwatani International Corporation (Europe) GmbH

PRODUCT(S): Gas cooker, Multi teppan plate, Sukiyaki nabe, Yakiniku grill, Takoyaki plate
ADDRESS: Immermannstrasse, 40 · D-40210, Dusseldorf, Germany
TEL: +49-(0)211-166-660
FAX: +49-(0)211-166-6623
E-MAIL: enosawa@iwatani.co.jp
WEB: http://www.iwatani.co.jp
DISTRIBUTION: JFC UK ☞See p.74

Hocho
Japanese Knives

JKC Ltd.

PRODUCT(S): Fine Japanese knife, Sharpening system
ADDRESS: 131-179 Belsize Rd. London NW6 4AQ UK
TEL: +44-(0)171-624-0436
FAX: +44-(0)171-624-9787
E-MAIL: general@jkcl.co.uk
WEB: http://www.japaneseknifecompany.com
DISTRIBUTION: Contact company directly

Wasyoku Kigu
Japanese Kitchenware

CNB Enterprises Oriental Products

PRODUCT(S): Porcelain ware, Lacquer work, Kitchen equipment, Chopsticks, Sushi robot
ADDRESS: Hazenkoog 17D 1822 BS Alkmaar Holland/P.O. Box 25 1860 AA Bergen NH Holland
TEL: +31-(0)72-5617635
FAX: +31-(0)72-5616187
E-MAIL: cnb.oriental@wxs.nl
WEB: http://www.cnboriental.nl
DISTRIBUTION: Contact company directly

CNB Enterprises, a leading specialist in oriental products, with sales, contacts and partners across the world. CNB Enterprises started as a company in1970 trading solely in pharmaceutical products from the Far East. The company has now expanded to become a general

importer and exporter of Japanese products, for example, porcelain ware, arts and crafts, kitchen equipment, lacquer work and kimonos. CNB Enterprises is working with renowned Japanese companies, selecting products for its high quality and style. CNB Enterprises has contacts all over the world.

Typhoon Ltd.

PRODUCT(S): Tableware, Lacquerware, Uniforms
ADDRESS: Unit K, Colindale Business Park, Carlisle Rd. London NW9 0HN UK
TEL: +44-(0)20-8200-5688
FAX: +44-(0)20-8205-5088
E-MAIL: typhoonltd@btclick.com
WEB: N/A
DISTRIBUTION: Contact company directly

Typhoon Ltd. provides a wide selection of Itamae supplies, an excellent range of Japanese tableware, lacquerware, uniforms and more. As a major supplier to restaurants and hotels, Typhoon stocks a range of round, oblong and square plates, bowls and dishes, trays, teacups, teapots, sake bottles and cups all in a variety of colours and designs. The company also stocks obento boxes, wooden hangiri, sushi boats, sushi oke, lanterns, norens, maneki neko, etc. Not only can you view all these and other products at its London showroom, but also Typhoon offers cash-and-carry and delivery services.

Waribashi
Disposable Chopsticks

New Star International Co., Ltd.

PRODUCT(S): Disposable chopsticks (Bamboo, Wooden)
ADDRESS: Unit 16, Cumberland Business Park, Cumberland Ave. Park Royal, London NW10 7RT UK
TEL: +44-(0)20-8838-1833
FAX: +44-(0)20-8965-1887

E-MAIL: N/A
WEB: N/A
DISTRIBUTION: Contact company directly

As an importer of disposable wooden and bamboo chopsticks, New Star aims to change the image of the chopstick characterised by the traditional plastic chopstick which is made unhygienic by repeated use. New Star stock all types of disposable chopsticks, from the basic and economical to the luxurious. Each pair of New Star chopsticks comes wrapped in a paper sleeve that can be custom designed to cater to the needs of the individual customer. Having established a reputation for practicality, hygiene and convenience, New Star's products are widely used in the Sushi bar, Noodle bar and oriental restaurant trades.

Sushi Robotto
Sushi Making Machine

Skerman Promac Ltd.

PRODUCT(S): Sushi & Norimaki robot, Nigiri robot, Rice cooker, Rice washer, Vegetable shredder, Rice mixer, Rice burger system, Maki cutter
ADDRESS: 162 Windmill Rd. West, Sunbury on Thames TW16 7HB UK
TEL: +44-(0)1932-789646
FAX: +44-(0)1932-761830
E-MAIL: troys@skerman.com
WEB: http://www.skermanpromac.com
DISTRIBUTION: Contact company directly

Suzumo Machinery Co., Ltd., the market leader in Japan, supplies Sushi-making equipment to small take-away shops, Kaiten conveyor style restaurants and factories. Skerman Promac Ltd. is the authorized distributor to Suzumo Machinery in the UK, Ireland and France. Suzumo's products are made in Japan and include rice washing machines, cooking, mixing, forming and wrapping implements. All types of sushi can be made using their equipment from Nigiri, Gunkan, Norimaki, 'California rolls' or inside out rolls, Onigiri, Oshizushi and the new 'Sushi Sandwich'. Their equipment is designed to produce good quality Sushi, increasing your output and profit while reducing production time.

DISTRIBUTORS

Distributors

Charles Wells Ltd.

ADDRESS: The Eagle Brewery, Havelock St. Bedford MK40 4LU UK
TEL: +44-(0)1234-272766
FAX: +44-(0)1234-279000
E-MAIL: N/A
WEB: http://www.charleswells.co.uk

Coors Brewers Ltd.

ADDRESS: 137 High St. Burton-on-Trent DE14 1JZ UK
TEL: +44-(0)1283-511000
FAX: +44-(0)1283-513353
E-MAIL: N/A
WEB: http://www.coorsbrewers.com

Harro Foods Ltd.

ADDRESS: 23A Lombard Rd. Merton, London SW19 3TZ UK
TEL: +44-(0)20-8543-3343
FAX: +44-(0)20-8542-1962
E-MAIL: ikubo@harro.co.uk
WEB: http://www.harro.co.uk

JFC (UK) Ltd.

ADDRESS: Unit 3, 1000 North Circular Rd. London NW2 7JP UK
TEL: +44-(0)20-8450-4626
FAX: +44-(0)20-8452-3734
E-MAIL: jfcuk@jfc.co.uk
WEB: http://www.jfc.com

Marblehead Brand Development Ltd

ADDRESS: 17 Station Rd. Milngavie, Glasgow G62 8PG UK
TEL: +44-(0)141-955-9091
FAX: +44-(0)141-956-6345
E-MAIL: glw@marblehead.fsbusiness.co.uk
WEB: N/A

Okanaga Europe
(Japan Prestige Sake Association)

ADDRESS: 8 Rue Thérèse 75001 Paris, France
TEL: +33-(0)1-49-27-04-39
FAX: +33-(0)1-40-20-97-56
E-MAIL: okanaga@wanadoo.fr
WEB: N/A

Tazaki Foods Ltd.

ADDRESS: 2 Dundee Way, Mollison Ave. Enfield, Middlesex EN3 7NJ UK
TEL: +44-(0)20-8344-3001
FAX: +44-(0)20-8344-3003
E-MAIL: info@tazakifoods.com
WEB: http://www.tazakifoods.com

For any other general enquiries on this section, please contact;
このプロダクツリスト全般に関するお問い合わせは下記まで

Cross Media Limited.
66 Wells Street, London W1T 3PY UK
Phone: +44 (0)20 7436 1960   Fax: +44 (0)20 7436 1930
Email: info@eat-japan.com
http://www.eat-japan.com

Japanese Restaurants
/Retailers

日本レストラン／小売店

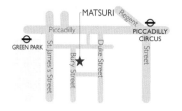

Greater London

Abeno

47 Museum St. London WC1A 1LY
TEL: 020-7405-3211
FAX: 020-7405-3212
E-MAIL: okonomi@abeno.co.uk
WEB: N/A

Akasaka

10A Golders Green Rd. London NW11 8LL
TEL: 020-8455-0676
FAX: N/A
E-MAIL: N/A
WEB: N/A

Aki Izakaya

182 Gray's Inn Rd. London WC1X 8EW
TEL: 020-7837-9281
FAX: 020-7837-9968
E-MAIL: demae@akidemae.com
WEB: http://www.akidemae.com

Asakusa

265 Eversholt St. London NW1 1BA
TEL: 020-7388-8533
FAX: 020-7388-7589
E-MAIL: N/A
WEB: N/A

Asta

Beaufort House, 5 Middlesex St. London E1 7AA
TEL: 020-7247-7065
FAX: 020-7377-8924
E-MAIL: info@asta-uk.co.uk
WEB: http://www.asta-uk.co.uk

Aykoku-Kaku

9 Walbrook, London EC4 8DQ
TEL: 020-7236-9020
FAX: 020-7489-8040
E-MAIL: N/A
WEB: http://www.japanweb.co.uk/ak

Aykoku-Kaku is one of the oldest Japanese restaurants in London. Situated in Bank, it is well known among top businesses and the decor is clean, spacious and simple. The restaurant boasts a full repertoire of Japanese food, from Sushi and Sashimi to Teppanyaki, noodle dishes and Donburi (rice bowls); there are also special set business lunches. It seats up to one hundred people and larger functions are occasionally organized. Kaiseki, Japanese 'nouvelle cuisine', can be delivered for external business functions or catering. With outstanding food and generous portions, this is a must for lovers of Japanese food.

Bar Japan

251a Old Brompton Rd. London SW5 9HP
TEL: 020-7370-2323
FAX: N/A
E-MAIL: N/A
WEB: N/A

Benihana (Piccadilly)

37 Sackville St. London W1S 3DQ
TEL: 020-7494-2525
FAX: 020-7494-1456
E-MAIL: benihana@dircon.co.uk
WEB: http://www.benihana.co.uk

We have nothing to hide at Benihana, our kitchen is your table. The three London locations Piccadilly, Chelsea and Swiss Cottage offer a unique way of eating out. Chefs dazzle you whilst cooking a variety of fine steak, vegetables and fresh seafood in front of your very eyes at your teppan table. The Teppanyaki menu offers great value for money, as each meal is served complete with accompaniments: 4 course lunch menus begin from just £8.75 and 6 course dinner menus begin from just £17.00. Each of the three restaurants also offers an a la carte Sushi menu which is available for guests during lunch and dinner.

Benihana (Chelsea)

77 King's Rd. London SW3 4NX
TEL: 020-7376-7799
FAX: 020-7376-7377
E-MAIL: benihana@dircon.co.uk
WEB: http://www.benihana.co.uk

Benihana (Swiss Cottage)

100 Avenue Rd. London NW3 3HF
TEL: 020-7586-9508
FAX: 020-7586-6740
E-MAIL: benihana@dircon.co.uk
WEB: http://www.benihana.co.uk

Bento

70-72 Clapham Park Rd. London SW4 7BX
TEL: 020-7622-3456
FAX: 020-8679-1602
E-MAIL: N/A
WEB: http://www.bento.co.uk

Cafe Japan

626 Finchley Rd. London NW11 7RR
TEL: 020-8455-6854
FAX: 020-8455-6854
E-MAIL: N/A
WEB: N/A

Chisou

4 Princes St. London W1B 2LE
TEL: 020-7629-3931
FAX: 020-7629-5255
E-MAIL: N/A
WEB: N/A

Cho-San

292 Upper Richmond Rd. London SW15 6TH
TEL: 020-8788-9626
FAX: 020-8455-8634
E-MAIL: N/A
WEB: N/A

Co-Co Noodle Bar

2 Cranbrook Rd. Ilford, Essex IG1 4DJ
TEL: 020-8478-9801
FAX: N/A
E-MAIL: N/A
WEB: N/A

Dai-Chan

18 Frith St. London W1V 5TS
TEL: 020-7494-3878
FAX: N/A
E-MAIL: N/A
WEB: N/A

Daruma-San

356 Regents Park Rd. London N3 2LJ
TEL: 020-8343-2608
FAX: N/A
E-MAIL: N/A
WEB: N/A

Defune

34 George St. London W1U 7DP
TEL: 020-7935-8311
FAX: 020-7487-3762
E-MAIL: N/A
WEB: N/A

Donzoko

15 Kingly St. London W1B 5PS
TEL: 020-7734-1974
FAX: 020-7734-1974
E-MAIL: N/A
WEB: N/A

Edokko

50 Red Lion St. London WC1R 4PF
TEL: 020-7242-3490
FAX: N/A
E-MAIL: N/A
WEB: N/A

Feng Sushi (Chelsea)

218 Fulham Rd. London SW10 9NB
TEL: 020-7795-1900
FAX: 020-7795-1501
E-MAIL: N/A
WEB: http://www.fengsushi.co.uk

"If our fish was any fresher you would have to slap it!" is the slogan of this decidedly contemporary, cutting-edge sushi restaurant. They are famous for their delicious sushi dishes, such as prawn California roll and inside-out poached salmon futo-maki. Dishes are beautifully presented such as sashimi, tempura, udon noodle soup and green tea ice-cream. Vegetarian dishes include 'Nippon Duck' (8 pancakes of Crispy Tofu, Spring Onions Cucumber and Hoi Sin Sauce) and Vegetarian Spring Rolls. Feng Sushi serves sake, Japanese plum wine and a range of Japanese beers. Delivery and takeaway can be ordered from the website.

Feng Sushi (Kensington)

24 Kensington Church St. London W8 3LP
TEL: 020-7937-7927
FAX: 020-7376-9191
E-MAIL: N/A
WEB: http://www.fengsushi.co.uk

Feng Sushi (London Bridge)

13 Stoney St. London SE1 9AD
TEL: 020-7407-8744
FAX: 020-7407-8777
E-MAIL: N/A
WEB: http://www.fengsushi.co.uk

Feng Sushi (Notting Hill Gate)

101 Notting Hill Gate, London W11 3JZ
TEL: 020-7727-1123
FAX: 020-7727-1125
E-MAIL: N/A
WEB: http://www.fengsushi.co.uk

Fluid

40 Charterhouse St. London EC1M 6JN
TEL: 020-7253-3444
FAX: 020-7608-2777
E-MAIL: info@fluidbar.com
WEB: http://www.fluidbar.com

Fujisan

326 Balham High Rd. London SW17 7AA
TEL: 020-8682-1777
FAX: 020-8682-1777
E-MAIL: N/A
WEB: N/A

Fujiyama Noodle Bar

7 Vining St. London SW9 8QA
TEL: 020-7737-2369
FAX: N/A
E-MAIL: N/A
WEB: http://www.newfujiyama.com

Gili Gulu

50-52 Monmouth St. London WC2H 9DG
TEL: 020-7379-6888
FAX: 020-7379-9888
E-MAIL: N/A
WEB: N/A

Ginnan

1/2 Rosebery Court, Rosebery Ave. London EC1R 5HP
TEL: 020-7278-0008
FAX: N/A
E-MAIL: N/A
WEB: N/A

Gonbei

151 King's Cross Rd. London WC1X 9BN
TEL: 020-7278-0619
FAX: 020-7278-9537
E-MAIL: N/A
WEB: N/A

Hazuki

43 Chandos Pl. London WC2N 4HS
TEL: 020-7240-2530
FAX: 020-7240-0556
E-MAIL: sushihazuki@hotmail.com
WEB: http://www.sushihazuki.co.uk

Hazuki is a modern restaurant with a styl-

ish, minimalist interior. Situated in the trendy Covent Garden area, it has easy access to West End theatres. The restaurant is relaxed and sophisticated with a wonderful array of antique furniture and ornaments. Hazuki serves a broad range of popular authentic Japanese dishes including Tempura, Sushi, Sashimi, Tonkatsu (deep fried pork in breadcrumbs), Saba Shioyaki (grilled mackerel), and Noodle soups. All food is prepared using the freshest ingredients. The wine list is also extensive, including a choice of good sake. Hazuki has a private room seating 12 and a basement room which seats 24.

Hi Sushi (Hampstead)

16 Hampstead High St. London NW3 1PX
TEL: 020-7794-2828
FAX: 020-7794-7328
E-MAIL: N/A
WEB: N/A

Hi Sushi (Soho)

40 Frith St. London W1B 5TF
TEL: 020-7734-9688
FAX: 020-7734-9882
E-MAIL: N/A
WEB: N/A

Ichi-Riki

17B Strutton Ground, London SW1P 2HY
TEL: 020-7233-1701
FAX: 020-7222-5713
E-MAIL: N/A
WEB: http://www.ichirikisushi.com

Ichiban Sushi

58a Atlantic Rd. London SW9 8PY
TEL: 020-7738-7006
FAX: N/A
E-MAIL: N/A
WEB: N/A

Ichizen

54 Goodge St. London W1P 1FP
TEL: 020-7637-0657
FAX: 020-7323 3648
E-MAIL: N/A
WEB: N/A

Ikeda

30 Brook St. London W1K 5DJ
TEL: 020-7629-2730
FAX: N/A
E-MAIL: N/A
WEB: N/A

Located near Bond Street station in the heart of the shopping district, Ikeda has a surprisingly quiet and calm atmosphere. The restaurant is particularly known for its fresh sashimi and high quality sushi, and an extensive menu. A firm favourite is omakase ('leave-it-to-the-chef' course), where fresh, seasonal dishes are served - customers often do not know all of the items in this course beforehand. Traditional dishes include Salmon Roe, Chopped raw beef with egg yolk and soy sauce as well as Niku Jaga (a popular home-cooked potato dish). Fried dishes include Tonkatsu, a succulent pork steak deep-fried in bread crumbs, and a Tempura of prawns.

Ikkyu

67A Tottenham Court Rd. London W1T 2EY
TEL: 020-7436-6169
FAX: 020-7323-5378
E-MAIL: N/A
WEB: N/A

Inaho

4 Hereford Rd. London W2 4AA
TEL: 020-7221-8495
FAX: N/A
E-MAIL: N/A
WEB: N/A

Inshoku

23-24 Lower Marsh, London SE1 7RJ
TEL: 020-7928-2311
FAX: 020-7928-2344
E-MAIL: inshoku@orbix.uk.net
WEB: http://www.lower-marsh.co.uk

Iroha

31 Vivian Ave. London NW4 3UX
TEL: 020-8202-9005
FAX: N/A
E-MAIL: N/A
WEB: N/A

Ishi

33 High St. London SW19 5BY
TEL: 020-8946-0001
FAX: 020-8947-7155
E-MAIL: N/A
WEB: N/A

Itsu (Canary Wharf)

Level 2, Cabot Pl. London E14 4QT
TEL: 020-7512-5790
FAX: 020-7512-5791
E-MAIL: N/A
WEB: http://www.itsu.co.uk

Itsu (Chelsea)

118 Draycott Ave. London SW3 3AE
TEL: 020-7590-2400
FAX: 020-7590-2403
E-MAIL: N/A
WEB: http://www.itsu.co.uk

Itsu (Soho)

103 Wardour St. London W1V 3TD
TEL: 020-7479-4790
FAX: 020-7479-4795
E-MAIL: N/A
WEB: http://www.itsu.co.uk

Japanese Canteen (Holborn)

83 High Holborn, London WC1V 6LF
TEL: N/A
FAX: N/A
E-MAIL: N/A
WEB: N/A

Japanese Canteen (Mayfair)

5 Thayer St. London W1M 5LE
TEL: N/A
FAX: N/A
E-MAIL: N/A
WEB: N/A

Japanese Canteen (St. Paul's)

9 Ludgate Broadway, London EC4V 6DU
TEL: N/A
FAX: N/A
E-MAIL: N/A
WEB: N/A

Jinkichi

73 Heath St. London NW3 6UG
TEL: 020-7794-6158
FAX: 020-7794-6158
E-MAIL: N/A
WEB: N/A

Kam-Pai!

26 Penton St. London N1 9PS
TEL: 020-7833-1380
FAX: N/A
E-MAIL: N/A
WEB: N/A

Kiku

17 Half Moon St. London W1J 7BE
TEL: 020-7499-4208
FAX: 020-7409-3259
E-MAIL: N/A
WEB: N/A

Kiku is a very sophisticated split level restaurant designed in Japanese style. The fashionable 15 seat sushi counter is staffed by experienced chefs serving only the best quality fish, fresh from the market every day. In addition to the main dining area, there is a private room which is perfect for business meetings. The staff are friendly and happy to help you choose your meal. James Long has expertly compiled the wine list noting wines that complement the various dishes on the menu. There is a wide variety of set lunches with Kiku special menu being very popular at £12.00. There is also a very good selection of sake.

Kikuchi

14 Hanway St. London W1T 1UD
TEL: 020-7637-7720
FAX: 020-7436-9513
E-MAIL: N/A
WEB: N/A

Koi

1E Palace Gate, London W8 5LS
TEL: 020-7581-8778
FAX: 020-7589-2788
E-MAIL: N/A
WEB: N/A

Komatsu Sushi

40 Great Windmill St. London W1 7LY
TEL: 020-7287-5298
FAX: 020-7287-5298
E-MAIL: N/A
WEB: N/A

Koto (The Grange City Hotel)

The Grange City Hotel, 8-10 Coopers Row, London EC3N 2BQ
TEL: 020-7863-3700
FAX: 020-7863-3701
E-MAIL: City@grangehotels.co.uk
WEB: http://www.grangehotels.com

Koto (The Grange Holborn Hotel)

The Grange Holborn Hotel, 50-60 Southampton Row, London WC1B 4AR
TEL: 020-7242-1800
FAX: 020-7404-1641
E-MAIL: holborn@grangehotels.co.uk
WEB: http://www.grangehotels.com

Kulu Kulu Sushi (Soho)

76 Brewer St. London W1R 3PH
TEL: 020-7734-7316
FAX: 020-7734-6507
E-MAIL: N/A
WEB: N/A

Kulu Kulu Sushi (South Kensington)

39 Thuloe Pl. London SW7 2HP
TEL: 020-7589-2225
FAX: 020-7589-2225
E-MAIL: N/A
WEB: N/A

Kura

3/4 Park Close, London SW1X 7PQ
TEL: 020-7581-1820
FAX: 020-7584-7794
E-MAIL: N/A
WEB: N/A

K-10

20 Copthall Ave. London EC2R 7DN
TEL: 020-7562-8510
FAX: 020-7562-8515
E-MAIL: N/A
WEB: http://www.k10.net

K-10 'xpress

102 Wardour St. London W1F 0TW
TEL: 020-7494-6520
FAX: 020-7494-6525
E-MAIL: N/A
WEB: http://www.k10.net

Little Japan

32 Thurloe St. London SW7 2LT
TEL: 020-7591-0207
FAX: N/A
E-MAIL: N/A
WEB: N/A

Maki Yaki

149 Merton Rd. London SW19 1ED
TEL: 020-8540-3113
FAX: N/A
E-MAIL: makiyaki99@hotmail.com
WEB: N/A

Matsu

558 Mile End Rd. London E3 4PL
TEL: 020-8983-3528
FAX: 020-8983-3528
E-MAIL: N/A
WEB: http://www.matsu.uk.com

Matsuri (High Holborn)

Mld City Pl. 71 High Holborn, London WC1V 6EA
TEL: 020-7430-1970
FAX: 020-7430-1971
E-MAIL: eat@matsuri-restaurant.com
WEB: http://www.matsuri-restaurant.com

The creators of the famous Teppanyaki restaurant, Matsuri St James's, have opened a restaurant in High Holborn which launches a new concept in dining: authentic Japanese food in a contemporary setting which is accessible to the British. Designed in three parts - each with its own distinctive style - it comprises of a brightly lit dining section, an elegant Teppanyaki area and a state of the art sushi counter. Four different types of Japanese cuisine characterise the menu: Bento Boxes, A la carte dishes, Teppanyaki and Sushi. The layered Bento Boxes and the Steamed chicken genmai are two of the delicious options on offer.

Matsuri (St James's)

15 Bury St. London SW1Y 6AL
TEL: 020-7839-1101
FAX: 020-7930-7010
E-MAIL: dine@matsuri-restaurant.com
WEB: http://www.matsuri-restaurant.com

Minami

74 Richmond Rd. Kingston, Surrey KT2 5EL
TEL: 020-8546-6691
FAX: 020-8549-0656
E-MAIL: N/A
WEB: N/A

Misaki

43 Chamberlayne Rd. London NW10 3NB
TEL: 020-8964-3939
FAX: 020-8964-3959
E-MAIL: N/A
WEB: http://www.misaki.co.uk

This relaxed and spacious new Japanese restaurant in Kensal Green specialises in sushi. Their popular signature sushi "Misaki's Dream Roll" is an original maki-sushi. It also serves a range of popular Japanese dishes such as donburi (rice bowl), tempura, ramen and udon noodle soups, yakitori, and yakisoba. Misaki have a sushi trial set for just £5.95 and a vegetable sushi set for the same price. There are a fine range of sakes and the fish is always extremely fresh. Private Japanese-style rooms (with English seating) are available for meetings and family occasions, and there is a delivery service.

Misato

11 Wardour St. London W1V 3HE
TEL: 020-7734-0808
FAX: 020-7734-8038
E-MAIL: N/A
WEB: N/A

Miso Noodle Bar (Beckenham)

132 High St. Beckenham, Kent BR3 1EB
TEL: 020-8658-4498
FAX: N/A
E-MAIL: info@misonoodlebar.co.uk
WEB: http://www.misonoodlebar.co.uk

Miso Noodle Bar (Bromley)

10 East St. Bromley, Kent BR1 1QX
TEL: 020-8460-4678
FAX: N/A
E-MAIL: info@misonoodlebar.co.uk
WEB: http://www.misonoodlebar.co.uk

Miso Noodle Bar (Haymarket)

66 Haymarket, London SW1Y 4RF
TEL: 020-7930-4800
FAX: N/A
E-MAIL: info@misonoodlebar.co.uk
WEB: http://www.misonoodlebar.co.uk

Mitsukoshi Restaurant

14-20 Lower Regent St. London SW1Y 4PH
TEL: 020-7930-0317
FAX: 020-7839-1167
E-MAIL: lonrest@mitsukoshi.co.jp
WEB: http://www.mitsukoshi-restaurant.co.uk

Although this restaurant is located in a department store in Piccadilly Circus this traditional Japanese restaurant is surprisingly quiet and relaxed. There are western as well as Japanese-style individual rooms, along with the usual sushi-counter seating. In the evening Mitsukoshi serves seasonal kai-seki courses, shabu-shabu (thin strips of beef boiled briefly by the customer in hot water at the table and eaten with various dips), sukiyaki (sliced beef cooked at the table) as well as a wide range of ippin-ryori (single-item dishes). Pre-theatre menus and lunch-time set-meals are also on offer.

Miyabi

Great Eastern Hotel, Liverpool St. London EC2M 7QN
TEL: 020-7618-7100
FAX: 020-7618-7101
E-MAIL: restaurants@great-eastern-hotel.co.uk
WEB: http://www.miyabi.co.uk

Miyama (City)

17 Godliman St. London EC4V 5BD
TEL: 020-7489-1937
FAX: 020-7236-0325
E-MAIL: N/A
WEB: N/A

Miyama (Mayfair)

38 Clarges St. London W1Y 7PJ
TEL: 020-7493-3807
FAX: 020-7493-1573
E-MAIL: N/A
WEB: N/A

Momo

14 Queens Parade, London W5 3HU
TEL: 020-8997-0206
FAX: 020-8997-0206
E-MAIL: N/A
WEB: N/A

Moshi Moshi Sushi (Canary Wharf)

Waitrose, Canada Pl. London E14 5EW
TEL: 020-7512-9201
FAX: 020-7512-9685
E-MAIL: info@moshimoshi.co.uk
WEB: http://www.moshimoshi.co.uk

Moshi Moshi Sushi (Liverpool St.)

Unit 24 Upper Level, Broadgate, London EC2M 7QH
TEL: 020-7247-3227
FAX: 020-7247-3227
E-MAIL: info@moshimoshi.co.uk
WEB: http://www.moshimoshi.co.uk

Moshi Moshi Sushi (Ludgate Circus)

7-8 Limeburner La. London EC4M 7HY
TEL: 020-7248-1808
FAX: 020-7248-1807
E-MAIL: info@moshimoshi.co.uk
WEB: http://www.moshimoshi.co.uk

Musha

133 Uxbridge Rd. London W13 9AU
TEL: 020-8566-3788
FAX: 020-8566-3798
E-MAIL: N/A
WEB: N/A

Nakamura

31 Marylebone La. London W1U 2NH
TEL: 020-7935-2931
FAX: N/A
E-MAIL: N/A
WEB: N/A

Nambu-tei

209A Baker St. London NW1 6AB
TEL: 020-7486-5026
FAX: 020-7224-1741
E-MAIL: N/A
WEB: N/A

Nobu

Metropolitan Hotel, 19 Old Park La. London W1K 4LB
TEL: 020-7447-4747
FAX: 020-7447-4749
E-MAIL: N/A
WEB: http://www.noburestaurant.com

Situated in one of London's hip hotels 'Metropolitan', Nobu's restaurant has introduced the innovative "new style" Japanese cuisine in the first European opening of a Nobu restaurant. Drawing from his experiences in South America, Nobuyuki Matsuhisa combines traditional Japanese sushi with a twist of South American flavour. Dishes include sashimi salad with Matshuhisa soy sauce dressing, Hamachi sashimi with jalapeño and black cod in miso. Matsuhisa's head chef, Mark Edwards has worked in world famous restaurants and teamed up with Nobu to open this restaurant in 1997. Nobu now has 13 restaurants worldwide.

Noodles Republic

318 High St. Sutton, Surrey SM1 1PR
TEL: 020-8661-6165
FAX: 020-8642-8870
E-MAIL: N/A
WEB: N/A

Noto

2/3 Bassishaw Highwalk, London Wall, London EC2V 5DS
TEL: 020-7256-9433
FAX: 020-7588-5656
E-MAIL: service@noto.co.uk
WEB: http://www.noto.co.uk

Oishii

70 Streatham Hill, London W2 4RD
TEL: 020-8674-6888
FAX: 020-8671-5888
E-MAIL: N/A
WEB: N/A

Okawari

13 Bond St. London W5 5AP
TEL: 020-8566-0466
FAX: 020-8566-2010
E-MAIL: N/A
WEB: N/A

Onami

236 Blythe Rd. London W14 0HJ
Tel: 020-7603-7267
FAX: 020-7602-6176
E-MAIL: N/A
WEB: N/A

Osushi

47 South End, Croydon, Surrey CR0 1BS
TEL: 020-8681-1166
FAX: N/A
E-MAIL: N/A
WEB: N/A

Ribon

6 Holborn Viaduct, London EC1 2AE
TEL: 020-7329-3254
FAX: 020-7329-3254
E-MAIL: N/A
WEB: N/A

Ryo Noodle Bar

84 Brewer St. London W1R 3PF
TEL: 020-7287-1318
FAX: 020-7287-1319
E-MAIL: Ryo84@supanet.com
WEB: N/A

Sakana-Tei

11 Maddox St. London W1S 2QF
TEL: 020-7629-3000
FAX: 020-7629-2360
E-MAIL: N/A
WEB: N/A

Saki

82 Queensway, London W2 3RL
TEL: 020-7229-7377
FAX: 020-7229-2234
E-MAIL: N/A
WEB: N/A

Sakura

9 Hanover St. London W1S 1YF
TEL: 020-7629-2961
FAX: 020-7491-1541
E-MAIL: N/A
WEB: N/A

Sapporo Ichiban

13 Catford Broadway, London SE6 4SP
TEL: 020-8690-8487
FAX: 020-8690-4949
E-MAIL: N/A
WEB: http://www.londonrestaurantsguide.com

Satsuma

56 Wardour St. London W1D 3HN
TEL: 020-7437-8338
FAX: 020-7437-3389
E-MAIL: N/A
WEB: http://www.satsuma.com

This aesthetic, minimalist Soho restaurant

is one of the best Sushi restaurants in this area. A range of Sushi maki rolls are available for under a £5 including: Spicy Tuna Rolls, Vegetable California Roll and Satsuma Roll (chicken teriyaki with mayonnaise). There is also Sashimi, Ramen, Noodles and a variety of side dishes, such as Okonomiyaki (a Japanese pancake with mayonnaise and vegetable sauce). Unusual rice dishes include Yakiniku Gohan – grilled sliced Tasmanian beef in garlic teriyaki sauce. Traditional Bento boxes also make a delicious set meal. It is open for lunch and dinner every day.

Seto

19 Kingly St. London W1R 5LB
TEL: 020-7434-0309
FAX: 020-8371-9757
E-MAIL: N/A
WEB: N/A

Shogun

Millennium Hotel, Adams Row, London W1Y 5BE
TEL: 020-7493-1255
FAX: 020-7493-1255
E-MAIL: N/A
WEB: N/A

Soba (Poland St.)

38 Poland St. London W1F 7LY
TEL: 020-7734-6400
FAX: 020-7734-6464
E-MAIL: N/A
WEB: http://www.soba.co.uk

Soba (Soho)

11/13 Soho St. London W1D 3DJ
TEL: 020-7287-7300
FAX: 020-7439-9300
E-MAIL: N/A
WEB: http://www.soba.co.uk

Soho Japan

Ground Floor, 27 Romilly St. London W1D 5AL
TEL: 020-7287-0606
FAX: N/A
E-MAIL: N/A
WEB: N/A

Sumos

169 King St. London W6 9JT
TEL: 020-8741-7916
FAX: N/A
E-MAIL: N/A
WEB: N/A

Sumosan

26 Albermarle St. London W1S 4HY
TEL: 020-7495-5999
FAX: 020-7355-1247
E-MAIL: info@sumosan.co.uk
WEB: http://www.sumosan.co.uk

Conveniently situated near Green Park Tube, Sumosan offers quality Japanese cuisine in a tranquil setting. The eight course Itadakimase dinner menu (set menu) is reasonable priced and offers such delicacies as teppanyaki, mixed Sushi. The Sushi is tasty and fresh here, and there is a variety of non-sushi options such as the Durk teppanyaki. You can create your own lunch set menu out of side dishes, main dishes and sushi. There is an extensive a la carte menu. Sumosan shows commitment to quality, and you can dine. Lunch and dinner Monday to Friday and only dinner Saturday and Sunday.

Sushi Wong

38 Kensington Church St. London W8 4BX
TEL: 020-7937-5007
FAX: 020-7937-0670
E-MAIL: N/A
WEB: N/A

Sushi-Say

33B Walm La. London NW2 5SH
TEL: 020-8459-2971
FAX: 020-8907-3229
E-MAIL: N/A
WEB: N/A

Sushi-So -Take away (Chancery Lane)

12 Chichester Rents, London WC2A 1EJ
TEL: 020-7404-1161
FAX: N/A
E-MAIL: N/A
WEB: N/A

Sushi-So -Take away (City Thames Link)

8 Ludgate Circus, London EC4N 7LD
TEL: 020-7353-0637
FAX: 020-8573-1772
E-MAIL: N/A
WEB: N/A

Sushi-So -Take away (Covent Garden)

43 Endell St. London WC2H 9AD
TEL: 020-7240-7361
FAX: N/A
E-MAIL: N/A
WEB: N/A

Sushi-So -Take away (Gloucester Rd.)

29 Gloucester Arcade, Cromwell Rd. London SW7 4DL
TEL: 020-7244-9448
FAX: N/A
E-MAIL: N/Λ
WEB: N/A

Sushi-So -Take away (Mansion House)

51A Queen Victoria St. London EC4N 4SJ
TEL: 020-7332-0108
FAX: N/A
E-MAIL: N/A
WEB: N/A

Sushi-So -Take away (Mayfair)

17 Avery Row, London W1K 4BF
TEL: 020-7629-8914
FAX: N/A
E-MAIL: N/A
WEB: N/A

Sushi-So -Take away (Moorgate)

Moorgate Tube Station, London EC2Y 9AE
TEL: 020-7638-3866
FAX: N/A
E-MAIL: N/A
WEB: N/A

Sushihiro

1 Station Parade, Uxbridge Rd. London W5 3LD
TEL: 020-8896-3175
FAX: 020-8896-3209
E-MAIL: N/A
WEB: N/A

Sushiwaka

75 Parkway, London NW1 7PB
TEL: 020-7482-2036
FAX: N/A
E-MAIL: N/A
WEB: N/A

Tajima-tei

Unit 1, Dorrington House, 9-15 Leather La. London EC1N 7ST
TEL: 020-7404-9665
FAX: N/A
E-MAIL: info@tajima-tei.co.uk
WEB: http://www.tajima-tei.co.uk

Taka

18 Mill Lane, Carshalton, Surrey SM5 2JY
TEL: 020-8647-6851
FAX: N/A
E-MAIL: N/A
WEB: N/A

Taro -Ramen

61 Brewer St. London W1R 3FW
TEL: 020-7734-5826
FAX: 020-7287-7093
E-MAIL: N/A
WEB: N/A

Taro -Yakiniku

293 Finchley Rd. London NW3 6DT
TEL: 020-7794-0190
FAX: 020-7431-9519
E-MAIL: N/A
WEB: N/A

Tatsuso

32 Broadgate Circle, Broadgate, London EC2M 2QS
TEL: 020-7638-5863
FAX: 020-7638-5864
E-MAIL: N/A
WEB: N/A

Situated near Liverpool Street Station, this popular authentic Japanese restaurant is a favourite of businessmen. The design is based on the japanese concept of "shiki-sai", denoting calm, grace and elegance: from the delicate flower arrangements to the tableware - each dish a japanese potter's work of art. There are set and a la carte menus which include Tempura, fresh lobster, turbot and tender beef. The selection of Teriyaki is extensive along with vinegared relishes and salads. It is an excellent venue for business lunches, serving Japanese haute-cuisine and real Teppanyaki. There is a choice of Western, Japanese rooms and counter seating.

Temari

430 Kings Rd. London SW10 0LJ
TEL: 020-7352-0101
FAX: 020-7352-0104
E-MAIL: N/A
WEB: N/A

Ten Ten Tei

56 Brewer St. London W1R 3PJ
TEL: 020-7287-1738
FAX: 020-7434-2352
E-MAIL: N/A
WEB: N/A

Tokiya

74 Battersea Rise, London SW11 1EH
TEL: 020-7223-5989
FAX: 020-7223-5989
E-MAIL: N/A
WEB: N/A

Toku

212 Piccadilly, London W1J 9HG
TEL: 020-7255-8255
FAX: 020-7434-0313
E-MAIL: N/A
WEB: http://www.japancentre.com

This popular Japanese restaurant serves delicious dishes using organic vegetables, free-range organic chicken and eggs, and rice 'polished' daily on the premises. Highly recommended by British and Japanese customers, their dishes are always served within five minutes and are very reasonably priced. For example, curry and rice at £4.80, Katsu Don -a bowl of rice topped with crispy deep fried pork - at £7.00, Salmon Don - a bowl of rice topped with fresh salmon sashimi with oriental ginger sauce - at £7.00. 'Toku' is simply the perfect place for busy, health-conscious people to dine.

Tokyo City

46 Gresham St. London EC2V 7AY
TEL: 020-7726-0308
FAX: 020-7726-0306
E-MAIL: N/A
WEB: N/A

Tokyo Diner

2 Newport Pl. London WC2H 7JJ
TEL: 020-7287-8777
FAX: 020-7726-0306
E-MAIL: N/A
WEB: N/A

JAPANESE RESTAURANTS

Tomo

7A Hanover St. London W1S 1YS
TEL: 020-7629-6228
FAX: 020-7629-6228
E-MAIL: N/A
WEB: N/A

Five minutes from Oxford Circus, this sushi bar is conveniently situated for shoppers. Tables overlook the busy Hanover Square, yet the dining area has a natural, relaxed atmosphere. The menu offers a variety of unpretentious Japanese food, including a selection of sushi, sashimi and noodle dishes. There is a reasonable priced set menu of mini don-buri and udon/soba noodles. Unlike other Japanese restaurants in London, Tomo is open all day. We don't close between lunch time and dinner time. The sushi bar sells take away lunch boxes and there is a children's menu on weekends.

Touzai

147-149 Curtain Rd. London EC2A 3QE
TEL: 020-7739-4505
FAX: 020-7739-3703
E-MAIL: info@touzai.co.uk
WEB: http://www.touzai.co.uk

Tsunami

Shop 3, 5-7 Voltaire Rd. London SW4 6DQ
TEL: 020-7978-1610
FAX: 020-7978-1591
E-MAIL: N/A
WEB: N/A

Ubon

34 Westferry Circus, London E14 8RR
TEL: 020-7719-7800
FAX: 020-7719-7801
E-MAIL: N/A
WEB: http://www.noburestaurant.com

Udon Noodle Bar

74 London Rd. West Croydon, Surrey, CR0 2TB
TEL: 020-8686-0602
FAX: N/A
E-MAIL: N/A
WEB: http://www.udon-noodle-bar.co.uk

Wagamama (Bloomsbury)

4A Streatham St. London WC1A 1JB
TEL: 020-7323-9223
FAX: 020-7323-9224
E-MAIL: N/A
WEB: http://www.wagamama.com

Wagamama (Camden)

11 Jamestown Rd. London NW1 7BW
TEL: 020-7428-0800
FAX: 020-7482-4887
E-MAIL: N/A
WEB: http://www.wagamama.com

Wagamama (Covent Garden)

1A Tavistock St. London WC2E 7PG
TEL: 020-7836-3330
FAX: 020-7240-8846
E-MAIL: N/A
WEB: http://www.wagamama.com

Wagamama (Harvey Nichols)

Harvey Nichols, Lower Ground Floor, 102-125 Knightsbridge, London SW1X 7RJ
TEL: 020-7201-8000
FAX: 020-7201-8080
E-MAIL: N/A
WEB: http://www.wagamama.com

Wagamama (Haymarket)

8 Norris St. London SW1Y 4RJ
TEL: 020-7631-3140
FAX: 020-7631-3160
E-MAIL: N/A
WEB: http://www.wagamama.com

Wagamama (Kensington)

26A High St. Kensington, London W8 4PF
TEL: 020-7376-1717
FAX: 020-7376-1552
E-MAIL: N/A
WEB: http://www.wagamama.com

Wagamama (Kingston upon Thames)

16-18 High St. London KT1 1EY
TEL: 020-8546-1117
FAX: 020-8974-8190
E-MAIL: N/A
WEB: http://www.wagamama.com

Wagamama (Leicester Sq.)

14A Irving St. London WC2H 7AS
TEL: 020-7839-2323
FAX: 020-7321-0537
E-MAIL: N/A
WEB: http://www.wagamama.com

Wagamama (Soho)

10A Lexington St. London W1R 3HS

TEL: 020-7292-0990
FAX: 020-7734-1815
E-MAIL: N/A
WEB: http://www.wagamama.com

Wagamama (Wigmore St.)

101A Wigmore St. London W1H 9LA
TEL: 020-7409-0111
FAX: 020-7409-0088
E-MAIL: N/A
WEB: http://www.wagamama.com

Wakaba

122A Finchley Rd. London NW3 5HT
TEL: 020-7586-7960
FAX: 020-7586-7960
E-MAIL: N/A
WEB: N/A

This sleek, modern restaurant with mirrored walls has received much media attention. Wakaba's speciality is 'traditional Japanese food' and it aims to recreate an authentic Japanese flavour. The 'Edomae sushi,' uses fresh ingredients; Crispy fried tempura and juicy teppanyaki are also highly recommended. The a la carte menu offers a choice of rare cooked beef fillet with seasoning and sour soya sauce, sliced meat and vegetables prepared at your table and a Sukiyaki dinner. Last but not least, try the handmade maccha (green tea) ice cream. Reservation is recommended.

Wasabi

34 Villiers St. London WC2N 6NJ
TEL: 020-7807-9992
FAX: 020-7807-9993
E-MAIL: info@itchdesign.co.uk
WEB: http://www.wasabi.uk.com

Yan-Baru

22 Harcourt St. London W1H 4HH
TEL: 020-7723-4110
FAX: N/A
E-MAIL: info.yanbaru@virgin.net
WEB: http://www.yanbaru.co.uk

Yo! Sushi (Bedford Sq.)

Myhotel, 11-13 Bayley St. Bedford Sq. London WC1B 3HD

TEL: 020-7636-0076
FAX: 020-7436-4473
E-MAIL: N/A
WEB: http://www.yosushi.com

Yo! Sushi (Farringdon)

95 Farringdon Rd. London EC1R 3BT
TEL: 020-7841-0785
FAX: 020-7841-0799
E-MAIL: N/A
WEB: http://www.yosushi.com

Yo! Sushi (Finchley Rd.)

O2 Centre, 255 Finchley Rd. London NW3 6LU
TEL: 020-7431-4499
FAX: 020-7431-4992
E-MAIL: N/A
WEB: http://www.yosushi.com

Yo! Sushi (Harvey Nichols)

Harvey Nichols, 5th Floor, 102-125 Knightsbridge, London SW1X 7RJ
TEL: 020-7235-5000
FAX: 020-7235-5020
E-MAIL: N/A
WEB: http://www.yosushi.com

Yo! Sushi (Islington)

N1 Centre, 39 Parkfield St. London N1 0PS
TEL: 020-7359-3502
FAX: 020-7359-1567
E-MAIL: N/A
WEB: http://www.yosushi.com

Yo! Sushi (Poland St.)

52 Poland St. London W1V 3DF
TEL: 020-7287-0443
FAX: 020-7287-2324
E-MAIL: N/A
WEB: http://www.yosushi.com

Yo! Sushi (Selfridges)

Selfridges, 400 Oxford St. London W1A 1AB
TEL: 020-7318-3944
FAX: 020-7318-3883
E-MAIL: N/A
WEB: http://www.yosushi.com

Yo! Sushi (Trocadero)

19 Rupert St. London W1D 7DH
TEL: 020-7434-2724
FAX: 020-7434-2729
E-MAIL: N/A
WEB: http://www.yosushi.com

Yo! Sushi (Whiteleys)

151 Queensway, London W2 4YN
TEL: 020-7727-9392
FAX: 020-7727-9390

E-MAIL: N/A
WEB: http://www.yosushi.com

Yoisho

33 Goodge St. London W1P 1FD
TEL: 020-7323-0477
FAX: N/A
E-MAIL: N/A
WEB: N/A

Yokoso Sushi

40 Whitefriars St. London EC4Y 8BH
TEL: 020-7583-9656
FAX: 020-7583-9657
E-MAIL: N/A
WEB: N/A

Yoshi Sushi (Hammersmith)

210 King St. London W6 0RA
TEL: 020-8748-5058
FAX: 020-8748-9396
E-MAIL: N/A
WEB: N/A

Yoshi Sushi (New Malden)

41 High St. New Malden, Surrey KT3 4HJ
TEL: 020-8942-0219
FAX: 020-8942-5101
E-MAIL: N/A
WEB: N/A

This is a family friendly restaurant in South London, about ten minutes by train from Waterloo station. It is a refreshing combination of modern and traditional Japanese decor. It serves a variety of popular Japanese food: the popular tuna, pink fatty tuna meat, mackerel and horse mackerel are served as sushi or as part of a combination menu. Chefs use very fresh ingredients. You may expect sushi to be pricey; however the moriawase (combination of various sushi) is on offer from a reasonable £14. A vegetarian menu is also available. Look out for the special menu at lunch times and the takeaway service.

Yoshino

3 Piccadilly Pl. London W1J 0DB
TEL: 020-7287-6622
FAX: 020-7287-1733
E-MAIL: yoshino@yoshino.net
WEB: N/A

Yumi

110 George St. London W1U 8NX
TEL: 020-7935-8320
FAX: 020-7224-0917
E-MAIL: N/A
WEB: N/A

Zen Spice Market

Marylebone Station, Melcombe Pl. London NW1 6JJ
TEL: 020-7723-8890
FAX: 020-7723-9345
E-MAIL: N/A
WEB: N/A

ZENW3

83/84 Hampstead High St. London NW3 1RE
TEL: 020-7794-7863
FAX: 020-7794-6956
E-MAIL: N/A
WEB: http://www.zenw3.com

Zipangu

8 Little Newport St. London WC2H 7JJ
TEL: 020-7437-5042
FAX: 020-7437-5042
E-MAIL: N/A
WEB: N/A

Zuma

5 Raphael St. London SW7 1DL
TEL: 020-7584-1010
FAX: 020-7584-5005
E-MAIL: info@zumarestaurant.com
WEB: http://www.zumarestaurant.com

The newly opened Zuma bases its style on 'izakaya'- the Japanese tapas bar where diners can choose and share a variety of dishes from the 'robata'grill, the sushi bar and a number of side dishes and salads. The restaurant's design emulates the layout of a Zen Garden and the designers, Tokyo's Noriyoshi Muramatsu and 'Super Potato' , have created a variety of exciting seating arrangements. These include sunken, 'Kotatsu' tables for private dining and the semi-private 'Chef's table', also diners can sit by the robata grill and watch the activity in the kitchen. Zuma Bar serves several tempting sake, shochu and sake cocktails as well as classic cocktails, non-alcoholic cleansers and other drinks.

Rest of the U.K.

Ah-So

60 Prince of Wales Rd. Norwich, Norfolk NR1 1LB
TEL: 01493-663851
FAX: 01493-602475
E-MAIL: jvgrose@aol.com
WEB: N/A

Azuma

4 Byron Pl. Bristol BS8 1JT
TEL: 0117-9276864
FAX: N/A
E-MAIL: N/A
WEB: N/A

Bonsai

143 Montague St. Worthing, West Sussex BN11 3BX
TEL: 01903-213036
FAX: N/A
E-MAIL: N/A
WEB: N/A

Budokan (City/Bristol)

31 Colston St. Bristol BS1 5AP
TEL: 08708-377-300
FAX: 08708-377-349
E-MAIL: city@budokan.co.uk
WEB: http://www.budokan.co.uk

Budokan offer a unique yet informal dining experience. With three branches and more openings planned for 2003, they aim to be the most successful chain of pan-Asian restaurants in the UK. Their menu includes a range of Asian cuisine, with authentic dishes from Japan, Thailand, Malaysia, Indonesia and Vietnam. Their dishes are tasty, nutritious and good value, using only the freshest ingredients; there is also a strong emphasis on visual presentation. Booking is only necessary for groups of six or more, and a fixed price party menu is available. Budokan also have catering service.

Budokan (Clifton/Bristol)

First Floor, Clifton Down, Whiteladies Rd. Clifton

Bristol BS8 2PH
TEL: 08708-377300
FAX: 08708-377349
E-MAIL: @budokan.co.uk
WEB: http://www.budokan.co.uk

Budokan (Birmingham)

128-130 Wharfside St. The Mailbox, Birmingham, West Midlands B1 1RQ
TEL: 08708-377300
FAX: 08708-377349
E-MAIL: @budokan.co.uk
WEB: http://www.budokan.co.uk

Edamame

15 Holywell St. Oxford, Oxfordshire OX1 3SA
TEL: 01865-246916
FAX: N/A
E-MAIL: N/A
WEB: http://www.edamame.co.uk

Fujiyama

35-39 Bath La. Newcastle upon Tyne, Tyne and Wear NE4 5SP
TEL: 0191-2330189
FAX: 0191-2210333
E-MAIL: mail@fujiyamarestaurant.com
WEB: http://www.fujiyamarestaurant.com

Funki Sushi

6 Queen St. Lymington, Hampshire SO4 9NH
TEL: 01590-679919
FAX: 01590-679919
E-MAIL: info@funkisushi.co.uk
WEB: http://www.funkisushi.co.uk

Gashi Gashi

96 Cowley Rd. Oxford, Oxfordshire OX4 1JE
TEL: 01865-200789
FAX: 01865-726826
E-MAIL: N/A
WEB: N/A

Ginza Teppan-Yaki (Quorn)

10 Leicester Rd. Quorn, Leicestershire LE12 8ET
TEL: 01509-412807
FAX: 01509-412807
E-MAIL: N/A
WEB: N/A

Ginza Teppan-Yaki (Sherwood)

593-595 Mansfield Rd. Sherwood, Nottinghamshire NG5 2FW
TEL: 0115-9691660
FAX: 0115-9245724
E-MAIL: N/A
WEB: N/A

Higoi

57 Lenton Blvd. Nottingham, Nottinghamshire NG7 2FQ
TEL: 0115-9423379
FAX: N/A
E-MAIL: N/A
WEB: N/A

Ichiban

Phoenix House2, Queen St. Newcastle upon Tyne, Tyne and Wear NE1 3UG
TEL: 0191-2616946
FAX: N/A
E-MAIL: N/A
WEB: N/A

Ichiban Noodle Cafe (Dumbarton Rd./Glasgow)

184 Dumbarton Rd. Glasgow G11 6UN
TEL: 0141-3349222
FAX: 0141-3349666
E-MAIL: raymond.tsang@ntlworld.com
WEB: http://www.ichiban.co.uk

Ichiban Noodle Cafe (Queen St./Glasgow)

50 Queen St. Glasgow G1 3DS
TEL: 0141-2044200
FAX: 0141-2043999
E-MAIL: raymond.tsang@ntlworld.com
WEB: http://www.ichiban.co.uk

Japanese Restaurant

149 Cattle Market Rd. Northampton, Northamptonshire NN1 1QS
TEL: 01604-250688
FAX: 01604-250688
E-MAIL: N/A
WEB: N/A

Japanese Yumi

2 West Coates, Edinburgh EH12 5JQ
TEL: 0131-3372173
FAX: N/A
E-MAIL: N/A
WEB: http://www.yumirestaurant.btinternet.co.uk

Little Tokyo

24 Central Rd. Leeds, West Yorkshire LS1 6DE
TEL: 0113-2439090
FAX: 0113-2439090
E-MAIL: N/A
WEB: N/A

Miyabi

6 Cable St. Lancaster, Lancashire LA1 1HD
TEL: 01524-39452
FAX: 01524-848356
E-MAIL: N/A
WEB: N/A

Moshi Moshi Sushi

Opticon, Bartholomew Sq. Brigton, East Sussex
BN1 1JS
TEL: 01273-719195
FAX: 01273-719196
E-MAIL: info@moshimoshi.co.uk
WEB: http://www.moshimoshi.co.uk

Niji Sushi

25A Thistle St. Edinburgh EH2 1DX
TEL: 0131-2205254
FAX: N/A
E-MAIL: N/A
WEB: N/A

Nippon Kan

Longmoor Rd. Griggs Green, Liphook, Hampshire
GU30 7PE
TEL: 01428-724555
FAX: 01428-725036
E-MAIL: info@oldthorns.com
WEB: http://www.oldthorns.com

Normans

36 Call La. Leeds, West Yorkshire LS1 6DT
TEL: 0113-2343988
FAX: 0113-2343988
E-MAIL: N/A
WEB: N/A

Oki Nami

208 Church Rd. Hove, East Sussex BN3 2DJ
TEL: 01273-773777
FAX: 01273-719741
E-MAIL: info@okinami.com
WEB: http://www.okinami.com

Oko

The Todd Building, 68 Ingram St. Glasgow G1
1RU
TEL: 0141-5721500
FAX: 0141-5721500
E-MAIL: info@okorestaurants.com
WEB: http://www.okorestaurants.com

Sa Shi Mi

Lamerwood Country Club, Codicote Rd.
Wheathampstead, Hertfordshire AL4 8GB
TEL: 01582-833013
FAX: 01582-832604
E-MAIL: lamerwood.co@virgin.net
WEB: http://www.lamerwood.humaxuk.co.uk

Sakura -Teppanyaki

69-70 Crossgate, Durham, Durham DH1 4PR
TEL: 0191-3832323
FAX: 0191-3839990
E-MAIL: N/A
WEB: N/A

Samusi

Regency House/36 Whitworth St. Manchester M1
3NR
TEL: 0161-2790022
FAX: 0161-2790023
E-MAIL: N/A
WEB: N/A

Shogun Teppan-yaki (Birmingham)

The Waters Edge/Brindley Pl. Birmingham, West
Midlands B1 2HL
TEL: 0121-6431856
FAX: 0121-6431856
E-MAIL: shogunteppanyaki@btconnect.com
WEB: http://www.shogunteppanyaki.com

Shogun Teppan-yaki (Leeds)

Granary Wharf, The Canal Basin, Leeds, West Yorkshire
LS1 4BR
TEL: 0113-2451856
FAX: 0113-2451856
E-MAIL: shogunteppanyaki@btconnect.com
WEB: http://www.shogunteppanyaki.com

Shogun Teppan-yaki -Sushi/Noodle Bar

113/115 Wharfside St. The Mail Box, Birmingham,
West Midlands B1 1RE
TEL: 0121-6321253
FAX: 0121-6321253
E-MAIL: shogunteppanyaki@btconnect.com
WEB: http://www.shogunteppanyaki.com

Skinny Sumo

11-13 Carlton St. Hockley, Nottingham, Nottinghamshire NG1 1NL
TEL: 0115-9551032
FAX: 0115-9551032
E-MAIL: sksumo@aol.com
WEB: N/A

Sukiyaki

6 Spencer St. St Albans, Hertfordshire AL3 5EG
TEL: 01727-865009
FAX: N/A
E-MAIL: N/A
WEB: N/A

Sukoshi

Unit 2, Frogmore St. Bristol BS1 5NA
TEL: 0117-9276003
FAX: 0117-3778968
E-MAIL: N/A
WEB: http://www.sukoshi.co.uk

Tenkaichi

236 City Rd. Cardiff, South Glamorgan CF24 3JJ
TEL: 029-2048-1888
FAX: N/A
E-MAIL: N/A
WEB: N/A

Teppanyaki (Manchester)

58-60 George St. Manchester M1 4HF
TEL: 0161-2282219
FAX: 0161-7734252
E-MAIL: N/A
WEB: http://www.teppanyakijapaneserestaurant.co.uk

The Teppanyaki restaurants in Leeds,
Birmingham and Manchester are well established and are highly acclaimed in many
good food guides. The restaurants are a
combination of modern architecture and traditional Japanese interior design. Teppanyaki
is a unique culinary art that has established
itself as one of the favourites of Japanese
cuisine. The preparation and presentation
takes place before your eyes on a heated
steel plate. Other specialities are Sushi and
Sashimi. Dishes are beautifully presented by
the Kimono-clad waiting staff, who bring you
an authentic Japanese eating experience.

Teppanyaki (Birmingham)

Unit 301, Arcadian Centre, Ladywell Walk, Hurst St.
Birmingham, West Midlands B5 4ST
TEL: 0121-6225183
FAX: 0121-6878734
E-MAIL: N/A
WEB: http://www.teppanyakijapaneserestaurant.co.uk

Teppanyaki (Leeds)

Belgrave Hall, Belgrave St. Leeds, West Yorkshire LS2 4DD
TEL: 0113-2453345
FAX: 0113-2438894
E-MAIL: N/A
WEB: http://www.teppanyakijapaneserestaurant.co.uk

Yau's

18 Woodthorpe Rd. Ashford, Middlesex TW15 2RY
TEL: 01784-420131
FAX: 01784-420131
E-MAIL: N/A
WEB: N/A

Yoko's Teppanyaki

Aston Hotel, 7-9 Franklin Mt. Harrogate, North
Yorkshire HG1 5EJ
TEL: 01423-564262
FAX: 01423-505542
E-MAIL: astonhotel@btinternet.com
WEB: http://www.hotel-harrogate.com

JAPANESE RESTAURANTS

Japanese Food Shops

Arigato

48/50 Brewer St. London W1 3HN
TEL: 020-7287-1722
FAX: 020-7287-1722
E-MAIL: N/A
WEB: N/A

Atari-Ya Foods (Acton)

7 Station Parade, Noel Rd. London W3 0DS
TEL: 020-8896-1552
FAX: N/A
E-MAIL: office@atariya.co.uk
WEB: http://www.atariya.co.uk

Atari-Ya Foods (Finchley)

595 High Rd. North Finchley, London N12 0DY
TEL: 020-8446-6669
FAX: 020-8446-6728
E-MAIL: office@atariya.co.uk
WEB: http://www.atariya.co.uk

Atari-Ya Foods (Golders Green)

15-16 Monkville Parade, Finchley Rd. London NW11 0AL
TEL: 020-8458-7626
FAX: 020-8458-7627
E-MAIL: office@atariya.co.uk
WEB: http://www.atariya.co.uk

Japan Centre Food Shop

212 Piccadilly, London W1J 9HG
TEL: 020-7434-4218
FAX: 020-7434-0313
E-MAIL: info@japancentrefoodshop.co.uk
WEB: http://www.japancentre.com

In the very heart of London, the Japan Centre Foodshop boasts the U.K.'s widest range of Japanese food, drink and more: soy sauce, sake, sushi-take-aways, noodles, drinks, and Japanese tableware are just some of what they have on offer. Their fish is deliciously fresh, and their vegetables selected especially for Japanese dishes. You can also explore the numerous variations of soy sauce, wasabi and nori. If you are unsure about which product to buy, the friendly staff are more than happy to help you find what you want. Once you've discovered the Japan Centre Foodshop, you'll realise how varied Japanese food is!

Jasmin

Stanton House Hotel, The Avenue, Stanton Fitzwarren, Swindon, Wiltshire SN6 7SD
TEL: 01793-861777
FAX: 01793-861857
E-MAIL: N/A
WEB: N/A

Lotte Supermarket

26 Maiden Rd. New Malden, Surrey KT3 6DD
TEL: 020-8942-9552
FAX: 020-8336-2414
E-MAIL: N/A
WEB: N/A

Midori

19 Marlborough Pl. Brighton, East Sussex BN1 1UB
TEL: 01273-601460
FAX: 01273-620422
E-MAIL: info@midori.co.uk
WEB: http://www.midori.co.uk

Minamoto Kichoan -Wagashi

44 Piccadilly, London W1V 9AJ
TEL: 020-7437-3135
FAX: 020-7437-3191
E-MAIL: mail@kitchoan.co.jp
WEB: http://www.kitchoan.co.jp

This store has a relaxing, warm Japanese atmosphere like its counterparts in Japan. Located on the corner of Piccadilly, they sell "Wagashi" - traditional Japanese, fruit-based desserts, which are baked, boiled, sugar or jellied. These popular sweets date back to the Yayoi Era (BC300-AC300). The chief ingredients are rice flour, azuki bean jam and sugar with any combination of seasonal fruits and nuts. The Director, Takushi Okada, is proud of the fact that they have achieved a winning combination of a tantalising dessert that is also low in cholestrol. He claims that the dessert is the crucial part of a meal.

Miura Foods

44 Coombe Rd. Kingston, Surrey KT2 7AF
TEL: 020-8549-8076
FAX: 020-8547-1216
E-MAIL: miura@miurafoods.fsnet.co.uk
WEB: N/A

Momo-ki

1a Knutsford Rd. Alderly Edge, Cheshire SK9 7SD
TEL: 01625-581818
FAX: 01625-581818
E-MAIL: N/A
WEB: N/A

Natural Natural

1 Goldhurst Terrace, London NW6 3HX
TEL: 020-7624-5734
FAX: 020-7372-0402
E-MAIL: natural@natural-natural.co.uk
WEB: N/A

Oki-Nami

12 York Pl. Brighton, East Sussex BN1 4GU
TEL: 01273-677702
FAX: 01273-681085
E-MAIL: info@okinami.com
WEB: http://www.okinami.com

Rice Wine

82 Brewer St. London W1F 9UA
TEL: 020-7439-3705
FAX: 020-7434-0962
E-MAIL: N/A
WEB: http://www.ricewineshop.com

Setsu Japan

196A Heaton Rd. Newcastle Upon Tyne, Tyne and Wear NE6 5HP
TEL: 0191-2659970
FAX: 0191-2242397
E-MAIL: SETSU-UK@ma.kew.net
WEB: N/A

T.K. Trading

Unit 6-7, The Chase Centre, 8 Chase Rd. Park Royal, London NW10 6QD
TEL: 020-8453-1743
FAX: 020-8453-0606
E-MAIL: tktrade@uk.so-net.com
WEB: http://www.japanfood.co.uk

Yamazaki Bakery -Bakery

Unit A 18, Oriental City, 399 Edgware Rd. London NW9 0JJ
TEL: 020-8205-5569
FAX: 020-8200-7097
E-MAIL: N/A
WEB: N/A

Oriental Food Shops

Hang Hon Wong

Connaught Building, 58-60 George St. Manchester M1 4HF
TEL: 0161-2286182
FAX: 0161-2363988
E-MAIL: N/A
WEB: http://www.hanghongwong.com

Hoo Hing (Chadwell Heath)

Hoo Hing Commercial Center, Freshwater Rd. Chadwell Heath, Romford, Essex RM8 1RX
TEL: 020-8548-3677
FAX: 020-8548-3699
E-MAIL: enquiries@hoohing.com
WEB: http://www.hoohing.com

Hoo Hing (Enfield)

Lockfield Ave. Off Mollison Ave. Brimsdown, London EN3 7QE
TEL: 020-8344-9888
FAX: 020-8344-9889
E-MAIL: enquiries@hoohing.com
WEB: http://www.hoohing.com

Hoo Hing (Hackney)

Unit A, Eastway Commercial Centre, Eastway, London E9 5NR
TEL: 020-8533-2811
FAX: 020-8533-2810
E-MAIL: enquiries@hoohing.com
WEB: http://www.hoohing.com

Hoo Hing (Mitcham)

Bond Rd. Off Western Rd. Mitcham, Surry CR4 3EB
TEL: 020-8687-2633
FAX: 020-8687-2655
E-MAIL: enquiries@hoohing.com
WEB: http://www.hoohing.com

Hoo Hing (Park Royal)

A406 North Circular Rd. Near Hanger La. London NW10 7TN
TEL: 020-8838-3388
FAX: 020-8838-0818
E-MAIL: enquiries@hoohing.com
WEB: http://www.hoohing.com

Loon Fung

1 Glacier Way, Alperton, Middlesex HA0 1HQ
TEL: 020-8810-8188
FAX: 020-8566-8785
E-MAIL: N/A
WEB: N/A

New Loon Moon

9a Gerrard St. London W1V 7LJ
TEL: 020-7734-3887
FAX: 020-7439-8880
E-MAIL: newloonmoon@cs.com
WEB: N/A

Oriental City Supermarket

399 Edgware Rd. London NW9 0JJ
TEL: 020-8200-0009
FAX: 020-8200-0848
E-MAIL: N/A
WEB: N/A

The Oriental City Supermarket on Edgware Road is the largest Oriental supermarket in Europe. The range of Japanese food is so extensive that even native-Japanese feel truly at home. With a superb selection of sushi, fresh vegetable, and souzai (ready meal), it is an absolute must for the ex-patriot as well as Japanese food fanatics – you can find any item of Japanese food here. The supermarket also sells Chinese, Korean, Malaysian and Thai food. Within the Oriental City itself there is a gift shop, a bookshp, a tableware shop and a food court offering many delicious Pan-Asian dishes. Japanese cultural events take place here frequently.

Wing Yip (Birmingham)

375 Nechells Park Rd. Nechells, Birmingham, West Midland B7 5NT
TEL: 0121-3276618
FAX: 0121-3276612
E-MAIL: enquiry@wingyip.demon.co.uk

Wing Yip (Croydon)

544 Purley Way, London CR0 4EF
TEL: 020-8688-4880
FAX: 020-5688-8786
E-MAIL: enquiry@wingyip.demon.co.uk
WEB: N/A

Wing Yip (Edgware Rd.)

395 Edgware Rd. London NW2 6LN
TEL: 020-8450-0422
FAX: 020-8452-1478
E-MAIL: enquiry@wingyip.demon.co.uk
WEB: N/A

WEB: N/A

Wing Yip (Manchester)

Oldham Rd. Ancoats, Manchester M4 5HU
TEL: 0161-8323215
FAX: 0161-8330758
E-MAIL: Fenquiry@wingyip.demon.co.uk
WEB: N/A

Others

Japanese Shop -Gift

1 Westminster Arcade, Parliment St. Harrogate, North Yorkshire HG1 2RN
TEL: 01423-529850
FAX: 01423-874011
E-MAIL: seles@thejapaneseshop.co.uk
WEB: http://www.thejapaneseshop.co.uk

Typhoon -Tableware

Unit K, Colindale Business Park, Carlisle Rd. London NW9 0HN
TEL: 020-8200-5688
FAX: 020-8205-5088
E-MAIL: typhoon@btclick.com
WEB: N/A

Utsuwa-no-yakata -Tableware

Unit 22, Oriental City, 398 Edgware Rd. London NW9 0JJ
TEL: 020-8201-3002
FAX: 020-8201-3004
E-MAIL: tajimiuk@ma.kew.net
WEB: http://www.utsuwa.co.uk

This shop's chief aim was to bring a flavour of Japan to England when it first opened in London in 1993. It now sells tableware for all types of cuisine as well and prides itself on the versatility of its products. An example of this is the small dishes which double up as candle holders. The shop is based in North London in the famous Oriental City, a haven for a wide range of products from Asia, but it also has a website for those who live further afield. Great gift ideas include a porcelain five-piece dish set, a tea set and a four-piece porcelain sake set. A porcelain Lazy Susan with cover, and a porcelain vase on a cart make for more original gift ideas.

ORIENTAL FOOD SHOPS
OTHERS

22 different kinds of Soy Sauce
9 different kinds of Wasabi
17 different kinds of Nori

*We have the widest range of Japanese food
in the UK. Can't decide? Grab one of
our friendly staff and tell them what you're
after, and we'll do the rest. Gladly.*

**Basement, 212 Piccadilly London W1
020-7434-4218
info@japancentrefoodshop.co.uk**

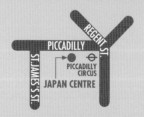

Index

索引

Published by Cross Media Ltd.
66 Wells Street, London W1T 3PY UK
Tel: +44 (0)20 7436 1960 Fax: +44 (0)20 7436 1930
www.eat-japan.com (Eat-Japan)
www.redbooks.net (Red Directory)
Email: info@eat-japan.com

Project Manager: Kazuhiro Marumo
Editor: Yoko Takechi
Assistant Editor: Chinatsu Sunaga, Fumiaki Tanaka
Art Director: Misa Watanabe
Designer: Kenji Kamiya, Rei Horie
Web Editor: Yasuyo Kimura
Advertising Manager: Mitsuru Togawa
PR Manager: Yukiko Takahashi
PR Assistant: Sonoe Sugawara
Client Relations Manager: Matt Motto

Special thanks to: Anna Davis, Shiho Hasegawa, Ayuko Hiruta,
Mizuki Imai, Yukie Kaizuka, Ian Lashley, Joanne Lawrence,
Fumiko Mihara, Tomoko Muroishi, Michael Nott, Serena Tarling,
Mary Thompson, Sari Uchida, STC